IMAGES OF WAR
THE FRENCH ARMY
AT VERDUN

A soldier grabs a quiet moment to write home. Béthincourt, July 1916.

IMAGES OF WAR
THE FRENCH ARMY AT VERDUN

RARE PHOTOGRAPHS FROM WARTIME ARCHIVES

IAN SUMNER

Pen & Sword
MILITARY

First published in Great Britain in 2016 by
PEN & SWORD MILITARY
an imprint of
Pen & Sword Books Ltd,
47 Church Street, Barnsley,
South Yorkshire.
S70 2AS

ISBN 978-1-47385-615-8

A CIP catalogue record for this book is available
from the British Library.

Typeset by Mac Style Ltd, Bridlington, East Yorkshire
Printed and bound in Great Britain by CPI

Pen & Sword Books Ltd incorporates the imprints of
Pen & Sword Aviation, Pen & Sword Family History, Pen & Sword Maritime,
Pen & Sword Military, Pen & Sword Discovery, Wharncliffe Local History,
Wharncliffe True Crime, Wharncliffe Transport, Pen and Sword Select,
Pen and Sword Military Classics

For a complete list of Pen & Sword titles please contact:
PEN & SWORD BOOKS LIMITED
47 Church Street, Barnsley, South Yorkshire, S70 2AS, England.
E-mail: enquiries@pen-and-sword.co.uk
Website: www.pen-and-sword.co.uk

Contents

Acknowledgements

I am grateful to my wife Maggie for all her help with the manuscript.

The photographs in this book come from the collections of the Bibliothèque de Documentation Internationale Contemporaine, Nanterre, France. I am grateful to the Bibliothèque and to the following known photographers:

Baehr: 6 (top)
Lieut Barbier: 8 (bottom)
Lieut Camondo: 57 (top), 75 (bottom), 78 (bottom)
Lieut Candlot: 12 (top), 36 (top)
Lieut Charbonnier: 83 (top), 92 (top)
Cordier: 19 (bottom)
Couturier: 23 (top)
G. Franjon: 9 (right)
Sous-lieut Guillaudet: 66 (bottom), 89
Capt Isoré: 13 (bottom)
Capt Jammes: 25, 35 (bottom), 37 (top), 76 (bottom)
Lapeyre: 39 (bottom), 52 (bottom), 68 (bottom), 81 (bottom)
Marius Plagues: 66 (top)
Sous-lieut Martin: 83 (bottom)
Capt Richard: 112 (bottom)
Royer: 54 (top)
Capt Toussaint: 35 (top)

The map of Verdun is from Wikipedia, drawn by Gdr.

Chapter One

No Longer a Role to Play?

On 13 September 1873, almost three years after the surrender of Verdun in the Franco-Prussian war, the last German troops of occupation in France marched out of the city. This former Roman fortress on the right bank of the Meuse, close to the border between France and the Holy Roman Empire, had been heavily fortified for centuries, and following Germany's annexation of Lorraine in 1871 had once again become a frontier city, perilously close to the new enemy forts around Metz.

In 1874 work began on a scheme designed by General Raymond Seré de Rivières (1815–95) as part of a barrier stretching from Dunkirk to Nice. Forts were constructed on the heights around the city, all sited to be mutually supportive and dug into the hillsides to reduce the size of the target presented to the enemy. A second phase of building in 1887–8 added reinforced concrete batteries to the existing forts, and 'intermediate works' (*ouvrages*) to cover the gaps and dead ground between them. Further work began in 1900, inserting thirty-four infantry shelters (*abris*) and four larger shelters (*abris-cavernes*) between the main forts. A number of steel gun turrets, armed with 75mm and 105mm guns, were also added in the first decade of the new century.

So on the outbreak of war in August 1914 Verdun was encircled by forty-four forts and smaller ouvrages in two concentric rings, all connected by a 60cm narrow-gauge railway line used for moving men, munitions and supplies from depots in and around the city. The most modern of the forts – Douaumont, Vaux and Moulainville – lay in the outer ring, facing north and east. The older examples, such as Saint-Michel, Souville and Belleville, were in the inner ring. Meanwhile the front line lay some kilometres in advance of the fortification line, in the wooded hills to the north – the Bois des Caures, Bois de Wavrille and Bois d'Herbebois.

Within days, Verdun found itself in the thick of the action. The French commander-in-chief General Joseph Joffre despatched his troops towards the German and Belgian frontiers to engage the enemy, only to see them driven back in a series of disastrous encounter battles. As Third Army retreated towards Verdun, its commander, General Pierre Ruffey, was sacked and replaced by General Maurice Sarrail. Ordered to attract enemy attention away from the Allied offensive on the Marne, Sarrail established his forces in positions outside the forts around the city, where he fought a series of bloody actions with the German Fifth Army. Pressed hard from east and west, the French line was bent almost double, creating a salient that penetrated deep into German-held territory. Joffre favoured relinquishing Verdun; he wanted to fight a mobile campaign, not tied down defending fortresses. Yet Sarrail refused to budge. Ever a political general, he presented himself to the press as the 'Saviour of Verdun', although his failure to prevent the creation of an enemy salient around Saint-Mihiel, cutting the major rail link to the south, in fact imperilled it still further. Sarrail was even touted as a potential commander-in-chief, but in July 1915 Joffre took pre-emptive action, exiling his rival to command the French forces in Salonika.

Over the spring and summer of 1915 the French attempted to force the invader from their soil in a number of bloody, failed offensives. Heavy fighting took place in the Argonne, west of Verdun, and the Woëvre to the south-east, but the city and its immediate environs remained quiet. Meanwhile the vulnerability of fortresses, and the men and matériel sheltered within, had become apparent to the French high command. The Belgian citadels of Liège and Antwerp had fallen quickly to the enemy guns in August 1914, while the important Austrian fortress of Przemyśl was captured easily by the Russians in October 1914, only for its defenders to retake it within a matter of weeks; the French fortress of Maubeuge held out for eleven days; Manonviller, outside Lunéville, for just fifty-two hours. In August 1915, desperately short of artillery, and in particular heavy artillery, for their renewed offensives in Champagne and Artois, the French commanders took the decision to strip the fortresses of their guns. 'The nation's defence is wholly dependent on its field armies,' argued General Yvon Dubail, commander of Eastern Army Group. 'The forts no longer have a role to play. Disarming them is the only way to obtain without delay the heavy artillery so urgently needed by the armies.'

At the fortress of Verdun, Dubail ordered the immediate redeployment of forty-three heavy batteries and eleven siege batteries. The forts lost all their movable artillery, 237 pieces, leaving just the guns installed in the turrets. A total of 647 tons of ammunition was also removed, greatly reducing the stocks available. The local commander, General Michel Coutanceau, denounced the decision – but to no avail. On 10 August Coutanceau was sacked and Verdun downgraded from 'fortress' to 'fortified region', the Région Fortifiée de Verdun (RFV). Its garrison – four infantry regiments, two chasseur battalions and a handful of artillery batteries, all raised from older reservists – became an element of XXX Corps, while responsibility for the sector was transferred from Dubail's Eastern Army Group to Central Army Group under General Fernand de Langle de Cary.

The new commander of the RFV was General Frédéric Herr. This former artilleryman immediately recognized the vulnerability of his new sector, lying as it did in a salient, surrounded by hills, in a valley liable to flooding, with poor rail and road links to the rest of France. And he was right to be concerned, for the Germans too had their eyes on Verdun. Convinced that the bloody failures of 1915 had fatally undermined French morale, the German commander-in-chief General Erich von Falkenhayn was planning to end the war on the western front with a single decisive blow. What he envisaged was not a breakthrough but a break-in, designed to capture high ground and force the French to counter-attack over a zone dominated by his guns – and the Verdun salient seemed the ideal place to implement his plans. His troops would launch a short, sharp attack on the right bank of the Meuse, seizing the ridges north-east of the city as far south as the Ouvrage de Froideterre–Fort Souville–Fort Tavannes line, and forcing the French to exhaust their reserves of men, matériel and morale in a series of costly, ineffective assaults. France would be compelled to sue for peace, obliging Britain in its turn to withdraw from mainland Europe, and leaving Germany free to concentrate all its resources against Russia in the east.

Herr immediately set to work reinforcing his defences, creating extra positions behind the main front lines on the ridges north of the city. However, his work failed to impress the commander of VII Corps, General Georges de Bazelaire: 'He handed me an artillery plan marked with innumerable concentric zones in green, yellow, violet, red and blue. It seemed fine on paper, but it was all show, just ideas. None of it actually existed on the ground.' After the war, commanders hastened to justify their action, or inaction, prior to the German assault. In this 'Battle of the Memoirs', de Langle de Cary blamed his predecessor for his previous neglect of the sector: 'how could I, over a few winter days, in rain and snow, make up for fifteen months of inaction?' But Dubail was having none of it: 'In the immediate aftermath of an all-out attack of the unprecedented scale and violence of that unleashed north of Verdun, the quality of the opposing defensive arrangements is irrelevant. I would even venture to say that the *abris* serve only to gather future prisoners in one place.'

In late 1915 French aerial reconnaissance missions began to notice an increase in railway traffic along the Meuse, as did French agents behind enemy lines. German deserters were also talking about a forthcoming offensive in the region. At General Headquarters (GQG) in Chantilly, the Intelligence Section duly recorded the information, but the Operations Section remained sceptical, arguing that Artois or Champagne were also possible targets. Joffre was equally reluctant to believe the reports: he could see no strategic value in the capture of Verdun and, besides, his attention was elsewhere – focused on planning his summer offensive on the Somme. As in 1914, the commander-in-chief preferred to base his conclusions on his own strategic preconceptions rather than the evidence placed before him. GQG grudgingly alerted XX Corps (General Maurice Balfourier) to prepare to occupy a position between Bar-le-Duc and Souilly, south of Verdun, should the need arise. Then on 23 January more troops were finally despatched to defend the sector: VII Corps (General de Bazelaire), XXX Corps (General Paul Chrétien) and II Corps (General Denis Duchêne) would hold the front lines, supported by a Central Army Group reserve five divisions strong – I Corps (General Adolphe Guillaumat) and XX Corps (General Balfourier), each with two divisions, plus the greater part of 19th Division.

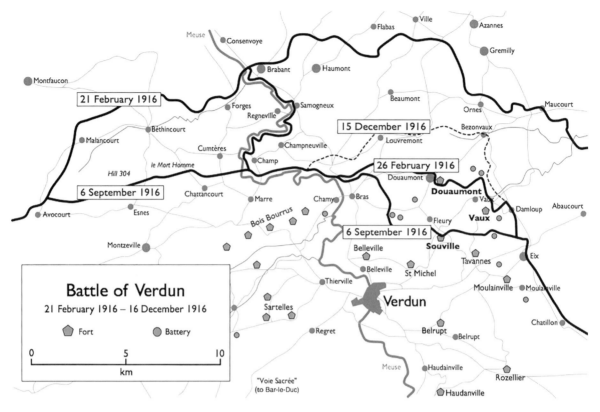

The battle of Verdun, 21 February 1916–16 December 1916.

General Joseph Joffre (1852–1931), commander-in-chief of the French army, is pictured at General Headquarters (GQG) in Chantilly, near Paris. An Engineers officer, Joffre rose to prominence after service in Indochina, West Africa and Madagascar. His unflappable temperament saw him through the worst days of the German advance into France in August 1914, and victory on the Marne that September sealed his renown. But the costly failures of 1915 soon tarnished his contemporary reputation, and his very imperturbability was later alleged to conceal a lack of real insight. The huge losses incurred at Verdun, and the subsequent failure of the Somme offensive to end the war, sealed his fate. He was sacked in December 1916 and replaced by General Robert Nivelle.

General Frédéric Herr (1855–1932) was appointed commander of the Région Fortifiée de Verdun (RFV) on 9 August 1915. Herr was an artilleryman who had served in the 1896 Madagascar campaign before distinguishing himself during the 1915 Champagne offensive as a corps commander around Les Éparges. The arrival of Pétain's Second Army in February 1916 further downgraded the status of the RFV. Herr made a brief return to a corps command in 1917, and in 1918 became Inspector of Artillery Training at GQG.

Fleury-devant-Douaumont, September 1915. General Coutanceau was not alone in opposing the decision to strip the Verdun forts of their guns. Politicians also voiced their disquiet, and in September members of the senate army committee arrived to inspect the city's defences. Senators Charles Humbert, Jules Jeanneney and Henry Bérenger are pictured here, left to right, alongside General Yvon Dubail (1851–1934), commander of Eastern Army Group. Absent is a fourth member of the committee, future French president Paul Doumer. Joffre resented political 'interference' on principle and rarely allowed it to influence his conduct of the campaign.

Fort Moulainville, January 1916. A working party sets out on a cold, damp winter morning. Situated east of the city, overlooking the plain of the Woëvre, Fort Moulainville was built in 1883, one of the second batch of forts to be constructed. Layers of reinforced concrete were added in 1905–9, and by August 1914 the fort was one of the most modern in the Verdun defences. It had room to house a garrison of 430 men, although on mobilization the actual complement was just over 300. The fort remained behind French lines throughout the battle but still within range of the German guns; it was hit by some 9,500 enemy shells.

75mm gun turret, Fort Moulainville, January 1916. Fourteen of these twin-gun turrets had been installed in the Verdun forts by 1914, housing heavily modified field guns capable of firing twenty to twenty-two rounds a minute at a range exceeding 4,600m. As a result of the modifications, the 75s were no longer usable in the field and were left in the turrets when the rest of the guns were removed in 1915. To the left is the cupola of an armoured observation post; to the rear, an open command post. Although damaged by a German 420mm on 6 September 1916, the twin 75s of the Moulainville turret fired almost 11,800 rounds during the battle.

155mm gun turret, Fort Moulainville, January 1916. The 155mm turret was equipped with a shortened field gun with a range of 7,500m. By 1914 just five had been installed in the Verdun forts: two at Moulainville, and one each at Douaumont, Rozelier and Vacherauville. Despite temporary damage to its mechanism from a number of direct hits, this Moulainville turret fired 5,833 rounds during the battle.

Command post, Fort Moulainville, January 1916. Heavily camouflaged under a layer of canvas and wattle, the post is equipped with a number of powerful telescopes. Among the group pictured here is a naval officer – the Verdun defences included several heavy artillery pieces crewed by sailors.

A visual signalling post, Côte 344, August 1915. Côte 344 lay on the right bank of the Meuse, beyond the outer line of forts north-east of the city, towards the Bois des Caures. Visual signalling worked by concentrating natural light, or the light of an acetylene lamp, into a tight beam. Many forts and posts used it as a back-up to voice and telegraph lines, often laid overground and thus liable to disruption. But in the smoke and fumes of battle visual signalling was no more reliable than fixed lines.

Fort Belleville, January 1916. An officer 'observes' the fall of shot through a trench periscope while training on a 240mm trench mortar. Although the 1915-pattern 240CT was the only French weapon capable of approaching the performance of the German *minenwerfer*, its size made it awkward to manoeuvre in a trench, leading to its replacement in 1917 by a longer-range version that could be sited further from the front lines. Belleville was one of the first forts to be constructed and lay behind French lines throughout the battle. When the Germans attacked in February 1916, it had been stripped of its armament and functioned only as a local command post.

Béthincourt, July 1915. A soldier grabs a quiet moment to write home. He is wearing a képi instead of the new Adrian helmet and is not wearing puttees, reflecting the relative calm of the sector over that summer, as front-line units had priority for both items of uniform. Letters were vital to maintaining morale among the troops: 'I'll be happy with a line, a word, an envelope with nothing inside, but write often,' begged one soldier. Béthincourt lay on the left bank of the Meuse, beyond the outer fortifications but just inside the front line. Already badly damaged in 1915, it was captured by the Germans on 8 April 1916 and completely destroyed in the subsequent fighting. By 1921 its pre-war population of 384 had fallen to just 51, and the modern village is just a scattering of houses.

A meal break in the streets of Béthincourt. On the right, a caricature of the French commander-in-chief General Joseph Joffre figures prominently among the graffiti decorating the wall. 'I imagine some future archaeologist … will write a voluminous monograph proving that these artworks date from the Stone Age, a period when mankind was not yet civilized and barbarism reigned,' wrote Charles Nordmann, a gunner with 5th Artillery. 'In fact they date from the Barracks Age, although regarding his second point the archaeologist will not be completely mistaken.'

Ornes, August 1915. The right-bank village of Ornes lay beyond the outer fortification line, north-east of Verdun. Many communities outside the defensive ring had only rudimentary defences: in Ornes, for example, these comprised little more than a loopholed wall across the main street. The wall displays a poignant advertisement for Denaiffe seed corn; the village was completely destroyed in the fighting and its fields would never safely bear crops again. In 1913 Ornes numbered 718 inhabitants; today just the walls of the church remain.

Vaux, January 1916. Vaux also lay beyond the outer fortification line, north-east of Verdun. The village occupied a key location at the junction of several valleys leading deep into the French positions. Here, the road entering the village from the east is barred only by a fence and some chevaux-de-frise. Fort Vaux is off to the left, while Fort Douaumont lies on the summit of the hill behind. Like Ornes, Vaux was one of nine villages completely destroyed in the fighting and later declared *morts pour la France* (died for France). The others were Beaumont, Bezonvaux, Cumières, Douaumont, Fleury, Haumont and Louvemont. Only Vaux was subsequently rebuilt. In 1913 the village had 287 inhabitants; today its population numbers just 70.

Champ, January 1916. A camouflaged pontoon bridge has been thrown across the Meuse near Champ, north of Verdun, to ease movement between the two banks of the river. The Germans were content to see the French infantry advance into the mouth of their guns and made no serious attempt to destroy any of the Meuse bridges.

Côte 304, January 1916. Côte 304 was a hill on the left bank of the Meuse, beyond the outer fortification line and west of the prominent Côte d'Oïe–Mort Homme ridge. While Joffre regarded the potential loss of Verdun with equanimity, General Herr was anxious to strengthen his defences wherever possible. Here men dig a last-minute shelter trench in front of an existing dug-out already well reinforced with turf and logs.

RFV Headquarters, Dugny, 31 December 1915. A German-speaking officer with the olive-branch badge of an interpreter on his collar interrogates a prisoner of Polish extraction. (Interpreters attached to the British and American forces wore a different badge, that of a sphinx). The intelligence provided by German prisoners was largely discounted by the French high command. The bearded man (standing, centre) is Lieutenant Louis Madelin (1871–1956). Madelin, a member of 44th Territorials, seconded to the staff, later became one of the first historians of the battle.

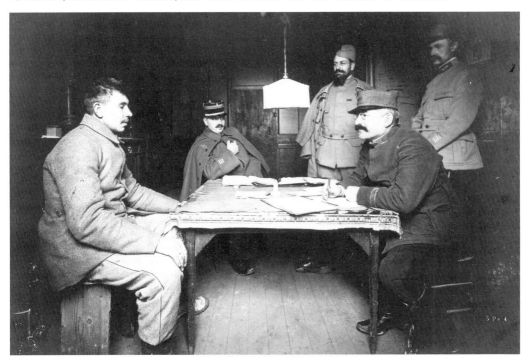

Fort Belleville, 4 January 1916. Hampered by dreadful winter weather, French reconnaissance squadrons failed to spot conclusive evidence of the German build-up. Captain Maxime Delafond (1879–1956), the CO of C18, is pictured (right) with his observer, Lieutenant Boinvillers, beside their Caudron G3 at the landing ground at Fort Belleville. During the battle, C18 was among the squadrons attached to XXX Corps. It flew a mixture of Caudron machines: the G3, by then fit only for use as a trainer, and the G4.

The weather also grounded the French observation balloons. Here a Type H balloon, a French copy of the German *Drachen*, ascends at Jouy-en-Argonne during the summer of 1915. Launching a captive balloon was a complicated affair. Each balloon had to be inflated, then 'walked' to its launch point by the ground crew: 'Supported 3 or 4 metres off the ground by teams of territorials, the big yellow cylinder – 26m x 7m – makes slow progress, crumpled, bloated, restrained by its ten tow ropes. Below hangs the rudder, limp and ridiculous. At the captain's chosen launch point, a long armoured vehicle, heavy, low-slung and full of machinery, waits to unwind the tough, thin cable attached to the balloon.'

Chapter Two

Stopping the Enemy at All Costs

At 7.15am on 21 February 1916 a German shell fell among the positions held by Colonel Émile Driant's 143rd Brigade (72nd Division) in the snowy Bois des Caures, beyond the right-bank fortification line. One shell was followed by a dozen, then hundreds, then thousands, fired by a total of 1,200 guns. For an hour the bombardment hammered the French front line between the Bois des Caures and the village of Vaux, before lifting to strike at areas in the rear, in a wide arc from the left-bank village of Avocourt to Les Paroches, over 30km south of the city. The impact was noticed even by an officer in the Vosges, some 160km away: 'I could feel the vibration quite clearly through the floor of my dug-out – a constant drumroll, punctuated by the rapid beats of a bass drum.'

Through the dense clouds of smoke and debris thrown up by the shells, French reconnaissance planes were unable to make out the action below. Then at 4.00pm the German infantry – part of the army group commanded by the Kaiser's son, Crown Prince Wilhelm – began moving forward on a 12km front. So churned up was the ground by the initial bombardment that in places the German units crossed the lines without realizing it; but if they were expecting their opponents to crumble, they were sadly mistaken. Elsewhere, recovering from the initial shock, the defenders offered desperate resistance. The incessant action quickly reduced 72nd Division to a handful of survivors and soon began to take a similar toll of the neighbouring 51st. Reinforcements were flung into the gaps with orders to counter-attack if possible, or at the very least to hold on to the last man. Their sacrifice slowed down the attack, but no more. German progress was relentless, and Herr – supported by de Langle de Cary – began making plans to evacuate the entire right bank, issuing the garrisons with explosives to blow up the forts rather than deliver them intact into enemy hands.

Alarmed by the reports arriving from Verdun, Joffre despatched his chief of staff, General Noël Édouard de Castelnau, to report first hand on the situation. As in 1914, Joffre's initial inclination was to abandon the city, but de Castelnau would have none of it. 'We must defend the Meuse on the right bank,' he proclaimed. 'We must stop the enemy [there] at all costs. There is no alternative.' In a hurriedly arranged conference at Chantilly on 24 February, President Raymond Poincaré and Prime Minister Aristide Briand took the same view. It was also decided that the task of holding Verdun required a new leader, one untainted by the disaster of recent days – and the man chosen by Joffre was the commander of Second Army, General Philippe Pétain.

Pétain arrived the following day to news of a fresh catastrophe: Fort Douaumont had fallen. Built in 1882, and almost immediately rebuilt in reinforced concrete, the fort was one of the most modern in the Verdun system, a cornerstone of the right-bank fortifications. Nevertheless, all its mobile artillery had been removed in August 1915, leaving just three guns – a single-gun 155mm turret and a twin-gun 75mm turret. Even worse, Douaumont was significantly undermanned: responsibility for keeping the garrison up to strength had fallen through the cracks during recent changes in command, and the fort, built to house 485 men, was held by just 56 territorials. Herr was planning to blow up Fort Douaumont rather than defend it, so had despatched no reinforcements; the 155mm gun was jammed, and when a handful of bold enemy assault pioneers clambered across the shell-damaged glacis, the fort fell without a fight.

Pétain installed his new HQ in the *mairie* at Souilly, south-west of Verdun, out of range of the German guns. His first objective was to stabilize the front, constructing a defence in depth composed of a thinly held 'advanced line of resistance', backed by a stronger 'principal line'. To keep his troops fresh, he planned to withdraw to rest any unit that had spent eight to ten days in the front line or had lost over half its effectives, while for maximum flexibility in deployment he transformed his army corps into purely administrative formations, each responsible for a defined sector of the trenches. 'Firepower kills' was his motto, and to minimize casualties he aimed to make the artillery shoulder the main burden of the French reply. 'I spent my time constantly urging the artillery into action,' he later explained. 'When the corps liaison officers arrived at my daily briefings in Souilly and began describing in minute detail the fighting on their front, I always interrupted them: "Tell me what your batteries have been up to. Then we can move on to other matters." Initially, their replies were confused … but my obvious annoyance soon alerted the relevant staffs to my main concern … Following my orders, our gunners took the offensive, concentrating their fire in real operations, carefully prepared, inflicting losses on the enemy but not on themselves. "The infantry must believe the artillery has the upper hand and that our guns are there to support them!" I constantly reiterated.'

Pétain also appreciated the potential value of aircraft, which could play a vital role in gathering information on German troop movements and observing the fall of shells on enemy positions. Each army corps sector received its own aerial component: one army corps squadron, ten to fifteen machines strong, one or two smaller heavy artillery flights to spot for the big guns, two or three balloon companies, and one or two divisional squadrons – about fifty planes in all. The new system ensured continuity of command, improved internal communication and facilitated local intelligence gathering, in general functioning so well that it was retained for the rest of the war. At the start of the offensive the German fighters managed to restrict the work of the French co-operation squadrons, but their success would be short lived. In March, the French created a dedicated fighter wing equipped with the new Nieuport 11 biplane, a huge advance over the opposing Fokker, allowing them to wrest overall air superiority from the enemy and maintain it for much of the battle.

Following Falkenhayn's original plan, German troops continued south along the right bank of the Meuse. By 26 February they had wrested control of the Côte de Talou, the ridge dominating the valley north of the outer fortification line, and were threatening the neighbouring Côte du Poivre. Brushing off French counter-attacks over the following week, the Germans also managed to capture the village of Douaumont and to work their way off the Côte de Talou into the Meuse valley. By early March they had advanced 3km into the French positions along a 10km front, achieving their initial objectives but still nowhere near taking them all. Supported by heavy artillery fire from across the Meuse, French resistance had been unexpectedly fierce and German casualties were mounting. To Falkenhayn, there was only option: to extend operations across the river.

On 6 March the Germans unleashed a limited offensive on the left bank of the Meuse, designed to clear out the enemy artillery and smooth the advance of their main right-bank force. Launching their assault at 10.00am, the Germans made swift progress, using their positions on the right bank to enfilade their opponents. On the first day they gained a foothold on the main French position close to the Meuse – a ridge running south-west from the Côte de l'Oïe to the triple summits of the ominously named Mort-Homme. Next day they advanced two-thirds of the way along the ridge while the troops on the floodplain threatened to outflank it. Then came a change of fortune: on 8 March the French retaliated and a counter-attack by 92nd Infantry drove the enemy back towards the river.

Renewing their assault on 14 March, the Germans captured two of the three summits of Mort-Homme, but the North Africans of 73rd Brigade (2nd Zouaves de marche and 2nd Tirailleurs de marche) clung tenaciously to the third. Yet even the capture of Mort-Homme would not suffice to protect the Germans from the French guns. The only way to hold the position was by taking the next hill to the west, Côte 304, forcing them once again to widen their offensive, capturing the villages of Malancourt on 31 March and Haucourt on 5 April. Falkenhayn was fast being pulled into a more general offensive, draining his own reserves as fast as those of the French.

On the right bank, the next objective was Fort Vaux and the neighbouring village of Vaux. The Germans were repulsed on three separate occasions on 16, 18 and 30 March, but on 1 April they finally managed to take half the village. The following day a further assault, preceded by an eight-hour artillery preparation, saw the Germans briefly penetrate the Bois de la Caillette, where they threatened to outflank the fort before being driven off by the counter-attacking 74th Infantry.

After pausing for a week, the Germans resumed their offensive on 9 April with a massive barrage of HE and gas shells that again failed to prise the French from their positions. Pétain knew this was a critical moment and the following day issued a clarion call to arms: 'The 9 April was a glorious day for our forces. The furious assaults of the men of the Crown Prince were repelled right along the line. Infantrymen, artillerymen, pioneers and aviators all vied with each other in their heroism. The Germans will probably attack again. Let each be on his guard, let each do his utmost to secure the same success as yesterday … Take heart, we will have them!'

Bois des Caures, January 1916. A queue of men from 59th Chasseurs gather around their mobile cooker. These cookers were a recent innovation in the French army; before the war, rations had been issued raw for the men to cook themselves, which sometimes took up to two hours. Centralizing the cooking in this way (one mobile cooker was issued per infantry company) was certainly a more practicable approach in the trenches.

Lieutenant Colonel Émile Driant (1855–1916), January 1916. A politician, soldier and writer, Driant was the parliamentary deputy for the *département* of Meurthe-et-Moselle, one of the instigators of the Croix de Guerre as an award for valour, and author of several pre-war fantasy novels concerning a future war. As a politician and serving officer, he attracted Joffre's disapproval in late 1915 by stepping outside the recognized chain of command to warn the minister of war, General Gallieni, of the shortcomings of the Verdun defences. The German attack on 21 February found him in the Bois des Caures commanding the local reservists of 143rd Brigade (72nd Division) – two chasseur à pied battalions, 56th and 59th. He was killed the following day fighting outside his HQ.

Some stunned survivors from the Bois des Caures, February 1916. Each man holds his gas mask in a pouch in the 'ready' position on his chest. Driant's two battalions started the battle on 21 February with approximately 600 men each; by the following day 59th Chasseurs had been reduced to fifty-three men of all ranks, and 56th Chasseurs to sixty-five. 'So violent was the shelling that we emerged from our shelters unable to recognize the countryside that had become so familiar over the previous four months,' recalled Captain Séguin (59th Chasseurs).

The survivors of the attack on the Bois des Caures take stock during a pause in the action, February 1916. The two chasseur battalions were relieved on 24 February. 72nd Division never returned to the battle and would not see action again until the Somme on 6 July.

Bois des Fosses, 24 February 1916. Thrown into action to shore up the crumbling front line, a group of zouaves from 37th Division dig some hurried scrapes. 'We don't know where the enemy is,' the men of 156th Infantry were told. 'Advance until you meet him, then dig in where you stand.' The full weight of the initial German attack fell on the front line in the forested heights some 15km north of Verdun. Falling back from the Bois de l'Herbebois to the Bois des Fosses to avoid encirclement, the men of 164th Infantry were met by 'a straight line of shelling difficult to cross because HE and shrapnel shells were bursting continuously. Bodies were lined out along a front of 100m; most were zouaves.'

General Étienne Bapst (1856–1935), Bras, early February 1916. Bapst, second from left, was an artilleryman with a fine professional reputation. He had begun the war as artillery commander of XII Corps and took command of the ill-fated 72nd Infantry Division in October 1914. On 21 February he withdrew his battered troops from exposed positions in the village of Brabant, only for General Chrétien, commander of XXX Corps, to order him to retake them, by now in German hands. The attack failed and Bapst was held responsible. He was sacked in early March, the first Verdun commander to be scapegoated, and never received another appointment.

In this German photograph, French prisoners are about to be marched off to captivity. Several of the men are from 243rd Infantry (51st Division); on 21 February the regiment was in the front line facing the main German offensive in the Bois de la Wavrille. The 243rd was overwhelmed, losing 50 per cent of its men, and was disbanded later that summer.

Fort Belleville, 23 February. A battery of long 120s from 5th Heavy Artillery is obliged by the German advance to withdraw from its positions near the fort. The 1878-pattern 120L was an old-fashioned gun, limited by its slow rate of fire, but it was accurate and continued to give good service throughout the war. The large plates around the wheels were known as '*cingoli*'. Designed to spread the weight of the gun and keep it stable in broken or muddy ground, they were normally dismounted for travel – a clear indication here of the regiment's rushed departure.

The first refugees flee the fighting, February 1916. Verdun had suffered two previous waves of evacuation when the battle came close in 1914 and 1915. On 21 February 1916 the remaining 1,200 civilians were evacuated to Nixéville, south-west of the city, before being dispersed all over France. The *Bulletin Meusien*, published in Paris to allow the evacuees to keep in touch, mentions local people living as far flung as Saint-Tropez on the Mediterranean, Auch in the foothills of the Pyrenees, and Grenoble in the Alps, as well as Paris and its suburbs.

The first wounded, a mixture of chasseurs, infantrymen and gunners, arrive from the front line at hospitals in Bar-le-Duc. Two chasseur battalions, 2nd Chasseurs and 4th Chasseurs (306th Brigade, 153rd Division), were thrown in to hold the line on 24 February: 'covered by their advanced elements, the companies deployed without support of any kind, [their flanks] completely in the air,' noted the battalion history of 2nd Chasseurs. 'Facing such a well-equipped enemy, the opening rounds immediately revealed the weakness of their situation … The German artillery soon opened fire. It would be evening before our guns arrived; until then there wasn't a gun in the sector.' Both battalions suffered heavy losses and were forced to withdraw just two days later.

Artillerymen establish a battery position, Beaumont, early February 1916. Lying beyond the right-bank fortification line, Beaumont was another of the nine villages later declared 'mort pour la France'. By 25 February this position lay in German hands. Rushing forward 'like fools' to reinforce the front line, Corporal Edouard Bougard and his chums (208th Infantry) were caught amid fierce fire: 'the shelling redoubled in intensity; the din was hellish; in the Bois des Fosses, trees broad as half barrels tumbled through the air, scythed down like wisps of straw.' Despite the carnage, Bougard's most vivid memory remained that of the cold: 'the stone-cracking cold, my feet were like ice.'

Standing at 390m above sea level, the highest point of the ridge north-east of the city, Fort Douaumont commanded extensive views in every direction, here looking eastwards from one of the observation posts in the 75mm gun turret.

Fort Douaumont again, looking north. 'For anyone arriving from the north, Douaumont was an imposing sight. It certainly made a huge impression on the German soldiers arriving to attack Verdun in early February 1916. What a dominating position, said the newcomers. It must surely contain a large, well-armed garrison. Attacking it would be a huge undertaking. The result would be uncertain and losses high. The German officers had to work hard to counter the demoralizing effects of such remarks.' In the centre of the photograph, the twin hills of the Jumelles d'Ornes had been the scene of heavy fighting in 1914, but lay behind enemy lines on 21 February 1916. They provided the Germans with an ideal platform from which to observe the Bois des Caures–Douaumont sector.

Fort Douaumont, January 1916. The fort had already been damaged by shelling in October 1914 and February 1915. It was garrisoned by members of 44th Territorials, who 'remembered [their CO] Lieutenant Colonel Demange, sitting in the window of his quarters, reading his newspaper, ignoring the 380s and 420s that were landing nearby and tossing blocks of masonry in the air like wisps of straw … the lieutenant colonel lived up to his motto, which was later adopted by the 44th: "*Toujours gaiement quoi qu'il arrive*" [Keep smiling whatever happens].'

Fort Douaumont, January 1916. The main entrance to the fort had been damaged by the February 1915 bombardment. From 21 February 1916 Fort Douaumont was hit by a deluge of nearly 800 shells of various calibres. With the 155mm gun out of action, jammed in the retracted position, the 75mm turret managed some reply, but senior commanders had already decided to blow up the fort rather than defend it. The charges were set, but not lit, when the Germans arrived four days later.

Two men find a sheltered spot in the Haudromont–Caurettes sector, 15 March 1916. Although the wood and quarries at Haudromont were vulnerable to enfilading from Fort Douaumont to the south, they provided a defendable position that allowed the French to resist the German advance until May. 'The 95th entered the lines all mixed up with the other regiments from 31st and 306th Brigades,' recalled Sergeant Aucouturier (1st Battalion, 95th Regiment, 31st Brigade). 'Everyone moved forward blind and took up position in the same way … often unaware who, if anyone, was to their left or right … We set up partly in old battery positions with a few scattered shelters, and partly on open ground. No trenches, apart from a little scrape 40cm deep. Hard by the edge of the Bois d'Haudromont we found several abandoned heavy guns. Around the guns and shelters were plenty of shell-cases and crates which the men used to build a breastwork. They grabbed their shovels and tried to dig in behind this improvised fortification, but the frost-hardened ground refused to admit the blade. The wind howled. Snowflakes swirled. We were frozen to the bone.'

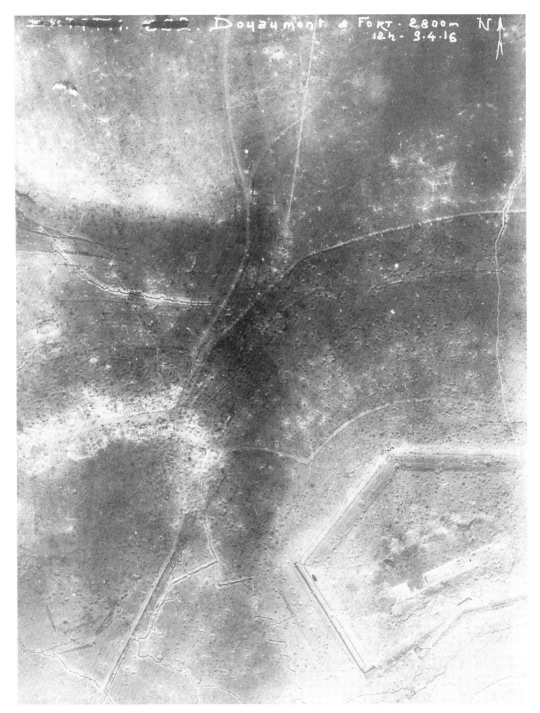

An aerial view of Fort Douaumont, taken by an aircraft of MF41, 9 April 1916. The white spots on the left mark the ruins of Douaumont village, obliterated in the battle. 'From the evening of 25 February,' commented General Joseph Rouquerol, commander of 16th Division, 'Fort Douaumont, under its new masters, was an active reproach to all who … denied the value of permanent fortifications, culminating in the pernicious order of 5 August 1915. Over the course of the war, abandoning Fort Douaumont was tantamount to losing 100,000 men.'

General Philippe Pétain (1856–1951). In August 1914 Pétain was about to retire as the colonel commanding 4th Infantry Brigade, where his officers included the young Lieutenant Charles de Gaulle (33rd Infantry). By the end of the month Pétain was commanding 6th Division, by October 1914 XXXIII Corps, and by June 1915 Second Army. The units under his command were distinguished by their careful training and thorough preparation. He was reluctant to attack with tired, demoralized troops, or without a marked superiority in men and particularly artillery – a cautious, methodical approach that set him at odds with the majority of his contemporaries, who preferred the bold thrust.

A medals ceremony, Verdun. Pétain took command of the Verdun sector on 25 February 1916. Here he is pictured, second left, alongside a number of his subordinates, all his contemporaries in the same class at Saint-Cyr, the *promotion* Plewna (1877–8): left to right, Colonel Adolphe Dehay (1858–1927), Colonel Adrien Famin (1857–1922) and General Bazelaire. Dehay and Famin had both been recalled to front-line service to command territorial regiments; de Bazelaire commanded VII Corps.

The first shells fall on French positions in the Bois de la Caillette, March 1916. The wood lay between Fort Douaumont and Fort Vaux, on the northern slopes of the Ravin du Bazil, a valley that led deep into French positions and controlled access to Fort Vaux from the north. The Bois de la Caillette was the scene of heavy fighting during March, and by early April it was in German hands. Ernest Barriau (17th Chasseurs) entered the trenches in what remained of the wood: 'A poignant detail, I couldn't say which unit we relieved because the only men still alive were those in my company. At Verdun, we relieved the dead.'

Trenches in the Ravin du Bazil, March 1916. On the left are the Bois de la Caillette and the Fort Douaumont ridge; on the right is the hill of Fort Vaux.

Bois de la Caillette, early April 1916. The men of 74th Infantry wait for the relief. On 3 April 1st Battalion advanced under fire on a two-company front, losing Captain de Visme, Lieutenant Morin, Lieutenant Légal and Sous-lieutenant Guigny, all killed. 'We could only advance further in bounds,' recalled Sous-lieutenant Jean Desmaires. 'The enemy barrage was very intense. Adjudant Moutier was wounded four times in the stomach. He leaned against a tree and prayed for an end to his suffering. His wish was granted: he was cut in half by a shell … Men were falling. Our losses were growing heavier by the minute. We advanced more than 600m [but] our objective was reached by a line of dead men.' Between 3 April and 6 April the regiment endured several heavy bombardments and counter-attacks as the Germans tried to secure the La Caillette plateau; by 8 April the wood was in German hands.

Fort Vaux, 12 March 1916. In this reconnaissance photograph, the village (top right) is already in German hands; the fort (bottom) still holds out. Two months later Captain Charles Delvert (101st Infantry) was holding a position in the Bois Fumin above the village: 'In the valley below, the main street of Vaux has been reduced to a heap of rubble and scorched beams, with a few very low fragments of wall. This little village, nestled in a valley, surrounded by woods and meadows, a tree-girded dam behind must once have been quite delightful. Now look what's left of it: bodies rotting in a jumble of ruins!'

Ravin des Grands Houyers, near Fort Vaux, January 1916. This well camouflaged position contains a 240mm naval gun, nicknamed *La Redoubtable*, manned by sailors under Lieutenant de Vaisseau Aubert. Although serving on land, the men are still wearing the wide-collared naval jumper and characteristic *bachi* cap with pom-pom. The gun was engaged on counter-battery work against a German 420mm in the Forêt de Spincourt, but by 25 February it was threatened by the German advance, forcing the crew to fire off their ammunition and blow it up *in situ*. They struggled to get the Bickford cord to light, but the demolition was successful and they were able to withdraw to safety.

Members of 2nd Mixed Regiment of Zouaves and Tirailleurs (48th Division) practise their gas-mask drill, May 1916. The regiment was heavily involved in the right-bank fighting between 25 February and 8 March, mainly around Douaumont village. Here they are wearing the M2 mask, introduced in December 1915. By the end of war 29 million had been produced. 'I've been too busy to write over the past few days,' Robert Pillon (24th Infantry) told his parents. 'The Germans attacked with poison gas on Monday night. The attack failed but we suffered some losses. What an awful way to fight. What a bunch of savages we have facing us.'

The men of 2nd Group, 84th Heavy Artillery, struggle to coax their vehicle into life in a snowy Bois d'Esnes, January 1916. The Bois d'Esnes lay outside the left-bank fortification line, south of Côte 304, and had remained relatively quiet until the Germans broadened their offensive in early March. By April the scene was very different: 'We left Esnes at dusk on 19 April to go into the front line,' wrote Pierre Joulain of 66th Infantry. 'How many dead on the way? It must have been hundreds. Leaving Esnes, we passed an entire platoon, gone to their eternal rest, every one blown to smithereens. Moving in Indian file, with all the halts forced on us by the shell-bursts, it took us until 2.00am to reach the sector and relieve the two or three poilus left alive. "Where are the Boches?" we asked. "Forty metres away," they replied. "You'll find out soon enough."'

Montzéville, January 1916. An unidentified German pilot, downed by anti-aircraft fire near Malancourt, is marched along the main street of this left-bank village, south of Mort-Homme. Like neighbouring Esnes, Montzéville remained behind French lines throughout the battle.

Fromeréville, January 1916. The village of Fromeréville lay further south again, some 10km west of Verdun. Here, a 155L gun passes through its streets. Despite its limited range and slow rate of fire, the 1877-pattern 155L remained the standard French heavy artillery piece throughout the war.

Bois d'Esnes, 1916. The cooks of 4th Battery, 84th Heavy Artillery, prepare food for Captain Jammes and his fellow officers. Rushing from positions around Toul on 23 February 1916, 4th Battery set up in the wood on 29 February. It spent the next few days shooting in the guns, then from 5 March to 20 March '[it] fired almost without interruption, day and night, counter-battery work but especially barrage fire' against targets in the Bois des Corbeaux, Bois de Forges and Bois de Malancourt. Using an observation post in the trees, the battery continued to engage targets of opportunity and undertake further counter-battery work before departing for the Somme in July.

Cumières, 10 March 1916. A sentry keeps careful watch beside a German corpse in the trenches outside the village, which lay below the Côte de l'Oïe–Mort-Homme ridge. 'The entire resistance line and battery zone looks like a slotted spoon,' reported VII Corps on the evening of 5 March 1916, the eve of the German attack. 'The shell-holes all overlap each other; the trench systems on the reverse [southern] slopes of Mort-Homme and the Côte de l'Oïe have been blown to bits.'

Bois des Corbeaux, 7.00am, 11 March 1916. Stretcher bearers struggle back with casualties. Léon Gestas (70th Territorials) was in position in this wood that lay in the dip between the Côte de l'Oïe and Mort-Homme summits. 'Shells were falling all around us,' he recalled. 'Men were killed without even knowing which direction the shot had come from. Rumours had spread among our men that the German bombardment would last a hundred hours and we were all on edge waiting for it to finish. But the deadline came and went and, far from abating, the shelling continued.'

As a matter of policy, French pre-war artillery production had focused almost exclusively on the 1896-pattern 75mm field gun which featured a revolutionary recoil mechanism, unique for the time, that greatly improved the rate and accuracy of fire. Although intended to engage targets at a range of 6,500m, the gun had a maximum range of 8,500m and maximum firing-rate of fifteen to eighteen rounds a minute. Its flat trajectory made it unsuitable for trench warfare, but with no viable howitzer in the order of battle, the field artillery regiments had to make do with whatever they could get their hands on.

A 155mm gun mounted on a railway chassis lends fire support near Béthincourt, 18 March 1916. The French had six such guns, originally destined for the Republic of Transvaal but never delivered because of the Boer War. They were given extra plate protection and mounted – three apiece – on two trains. However, the locomotives and other wagons remained unarmoured.

Ouvrage du Chana, 21 June 1916. The 155mm guns of 9th Battery, 85th Heavy Artillery begin a counter-barrage from their position close to this left-bank ouvrage, west of Verdun. Battlefield conditions hindered liaison between the artillery and the front line. 'On that evil April day, it was the turn of our artillery to plaster us for over an hour, with 155s too, sometimes a few metres behind our trenches, sometimes a few metres in front,' recalled Frédéric Bayon, 126th Infantry. 'Earth rained down on our heads, jagged lumps of red-hot shrapnel shot into the parapets; some even hit the rolled-up blankets on top of the pack I'd stuck on my head until the hail stopped; the closer the shells came, the louder the Germans laughed in their trenches 20m away. A continuous stream of red rockets went up, begging the gunners to raise their sights. Meanwhile in his dug-out the colonel was tearing his hair out. "The bastards!" he shouted. "They're targeting my regiment."'

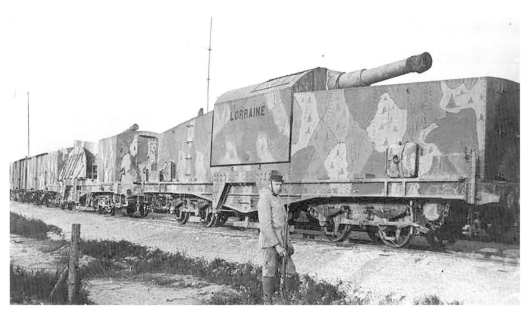

The exotically camouflaged 19cm railway gun *Lorraine*, Villers-en-Argonne, 31 May 1916. Twenty-six such guns were produced, using former coastal artillery weapons manufactured between 1870 and 1893. Depending on the type of shell, its range varied between 11,500m and 18,300m. The huge pre-war emphasis on field guns came at the expense of the heavy artillery, interest in the subject representing professional suicide for any aspiring officer. In the spring of 1915 the commander of one 19cm battery raised eyebrows when he requested thermometers and barometers to improve the accuracy of his guns, but with the advent of trench warfare, and the employment of naval gunners in the field armies, heavy – and then very heavy – artillery came into its own. The battle of Verdun proved its usefulness and the arm soon saw a dramatic expansion.

Inside the turret of the *Lorraine*, Villers-en-Argonne, 31 May 1916. The twelve-man crew worked in extremely cramped conditions, firing four shots every five minutes. They were accommodated in railway wagons and, appropriately for men serving a former naval gun, slept in hammocks.

Major Charles de Rose (1876–1916), France's leading fighter tactician, is pictured (left) with the commander of Fifth Army, General Louis Franchet d'Espèrey (1856–1942). Recognizing the importance of air superiority to victory in the battle, Pétain immediately had de Rose transferred from Fifth Army to Second Army. 'Clear the skies for me, de Rose! I'm blind!' Pétain told his new aviation commander on 28 February. 'Everything is settled with GQG. Everyone is at your disposal – at the rear and at the front – so you can organize things how you like. Nothing will be denied you. But get a move on! You can see the situation with your own eyes. It's quite simple. If we're driven from the skies, we'll lose Verdun.'

Sous-lieutenant Jean Navarre (1895–1919), Lemmes, 16 May 1916. Navarre, the so-called 'Sentinel of Verdun', was a prominent member of the dedicated fighter units created by de Rose to interdict German observation planes. Navarre obtained twelve victories in total and is pictured here about to take off in his red Nieuport scout. Eugène Louis (25th Chasseurs) was an ardent admirer: 'Lieutenant Navarre hated to waste a journey. If there was no prey about, he would use the return trip to entertain the men crouching in the trenches. He absolutely worshipped the poilus. When asked why he didn't keep count of his victories, he replied, "Is that what they do in the trenches? No! Then why should I be any different?" On his way back from a patrol, he liked to stage a bit of a show. He gave it everything, running through his entire repertoire to show us poor devils that we hadn't been forgotten and that he was doing his best to divert us.'

Vadelaincourt, 9 October 1916. Adjudant Maxime Lenoir (1888–1916), fourth from the left, and his fellow pilots from N23 are pictured in front of his plane, *Trompe la mort* (Death Defier) – a very early SPAD. Lenoir scored eleven victories in all. 'I didn't call my plane *Trompe la mort* for nothing,' he commented. 'I make light of death. It doesn't scare me. Life can be sweet but a good death is no less fine.' If the contemporary caption is correct, this photograph was taken only days before Lenoir was shot down and killed over Fromezey on 25 October 1916.

A demonstration of the rocket-armed Nieuport fighter, Le Bourget, 19 July 1916. These aircraft first saw active service on 22 May 1916, attacking the German observation balloons prior to an attempt to retake Fort Douaumont. The mission was successful, but it served only to alert the enemy to the prospective attack. The Germans reinforced their ground defences and the French were driven off. Lieutenant de Vaisseau Yves Le Prieur, the inventor of the rocket system, watched as the Nieuports took off from the airfield at Lemmes: 'The eight planes were ready at 4.00am on 22 May … and carried out the plan to the letter. At 4.50am six of the eight balloons were downed in flames in under a minute. Two misses were recorded: by Barault and by Boutiny. One pilot was reported missing: Réservat. He shot down his balloon but was hit by anti-aircraft fire. He escaped unhurt and managed to set fire to his plane on the ground.'

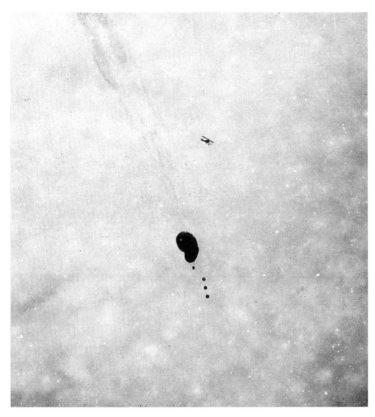

The Le Prieur rocket was a spectacular, if frequently unreliable, weapon. In this demonstration at Le Bourget, the path of the rockets is revealed by the trails of smoke heading directly towards the balloon, while the Nieuport climbs away to safety.

Vadelaincourt, April 1916. Aircraft played an important role in gathering information on German troop movements and observing the fall of shells. About to take off here is a Farman F.40 from F22, a squadron attached to XII Corps; a dedicated photo-interpretation section (51st) was added to the squadron during the battle.

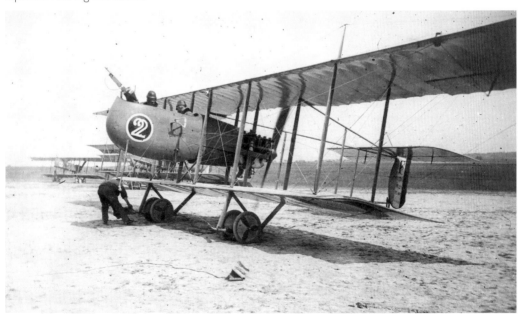

Vadelaincourt, May 1916. A member of the ground crew hurries away with the camera from the recently landed *Totote*, a Caudron G.4. To prevent vibrations from spoiling the image, the pilot had to stall his engine and then restart it – a task requiring great skill and no little sang-froid. By 1916 the camera was fixed to the fuselage, sparing the observer the perilous task of leaning over the side of the aircraft, buffeted by the slipstream, all the while holding the camera with its long, heavy lens. Roll film had also replaced glass plates, allowing each mission to take three hundred pictures rather than the original twelve, and the aircraft to spend more time over the target.

Vadelaincourt, 21 October 1916. The champion heavyweight boxer Georges Carpentier (1894–1975) and his observer, artillery lieutenant Fernand Wiedemann, were members of squadron MF8. They are pictured here with their Farman aircraft; the Lewis machine gun is a local enhancement. Wiedemann (right), who later became the CO of MF8, had one victory to his credit, shooting down a Fokker on 9 March 1916 while flying with Corporal Albert Baroz. Carpentier flew numerous bombing/reconnaissance missions over the Verdun sector in 1916. He later recalled that flying there 'was very difficult, because the weather was dreadful and you had to fly low. I came back in a plane riddled with bullets and peppered by stones from the ground.'

Lemmes, July 1916. The officers' mess-tent of F216, shortly after the squadron moved from Le Hamel, on the Somme. The cartoon shows a British officer eagerly pursuing a nurse. The caption above reads, '2 July 1916', and below, 'It's a long way to Germany, boys'. F216 was an artillery squadron, spotting the fall of shells for the guns of 85th Heavy Artillery, a regiment which operated under the direct command of Second Army.

Chapter Three

The Road Must Hold

On his arrival at Verdun, Pétain had immediately grasped the attritional nature of the battle. Victory could only be obtained through a huge logistical effort, supplying vast quantities of men and matériel to front-line positions around the clock – an enormous problem in a sector with so few road and rail links. The standard-gauge line south from Verdun had been cut by the Germans around Saint-Mihiel in 1914, and no serious attempt had been made to re-establish it or pinch out the salient. Meanwhile the only remaining standard-gauge line, running west to Sainte-Ménehould, lay within range of German artillery for part of its length and was almost unusable from Clermont-en-Argonne eastwards.

The only practical alternatives were twofold: a narrow-gauge railway running some 75km from Bar-le-Duc north to Verdun, and an undulating *route départementale*, the modern D1916, following roughly the same route. Neither had been built for military purposes. The railway line, part of the *Le Meusien* network requisitioned by GQG in December 1914, was designed to carry passengers and goods between local villages and towns; its infrastructure and rolling stock were inadequate and its capacity limited to some 400 tonnes a day. Improvement work was undertaken on all lines leading to the Argonne and Verdun during 1915 – platforms were extended, track laid and transhipment points constructed, telephones installed in all stations, and suitable rolling stock identified and requisitioned throughout France – and by the time the Germans attacked in February 1916 the *Le Meusien* line had been transformed. Its capacity had grown to some 1,600 tonnes and 1,500 passengers a day; extra spurs had been added to connect with the standard-gauge lines at Dugny; and the busiest stretches of track had been doubled. During the battle the line was used primarily to carry rations and fodder into the sector, dropping them at intermediate stations – Dugny, Nixéville, Lemmes, Souilly, Heippes, Beauzée, Chaumont-sur-Aire and Pierrefitte – where they were stored for pick-up by front-line units at any time of the day or night. By June it was moving on average 2,650 tonnes of goods and 1,500 men a day into the city and bringing out 930 casualties.

Work on a new standard-gauge line, later numbered 6bis, began in February 1916 and was completed in late June. It ran 57km from Nettancourt-Sommeilles, just north of the major railway junction of Revigny-sur-Ornain, to the depot at Dugny, 7km south of Verdun. Food and equipment was delivered to Dugny, then taken by lorry to a chain of smaller depots, each of which served one or more divisions. A spur to Clermont-en-Argonne, intended for railway artillery, was opened at the same time, allowing two 400mm howitzers to be brought in to fire on Fort Douaumont and Fort Vaux. A second spur to Dombasle-en-Argonne took longer to complete, finally opening on 25 September.

Until 6bis was operational, men, munitions and other matériel had to be moved by lorry. During 1915 the narrow country road linking Baudonvilliers and Bar-le-Duc with Verdun had been widened to 7m – sufficient for two lorries to pass each other comfortably, with room for a faster vehicle to squeeze through in an emergency – and its surface improved. Meanwhile, drawing on experience from Champagne and Artois, the Service Automobile already had vehicles in place and traffic management plans at the ready. On 22 February the road was placed under a single commander, divided into sectors, and horse transport banned. Thirteen battalions, mostly territorials, were allocated to keeping the road in repair; quarries were opened along the route to provide stone, and each sector was given its own maintenance crews and mechanics, available between 6.00am and 6.00pm under normal circumstances, but round the clock in conditions of ice, snow or thaw.

From an overall strength of 4,000 vehicles (around a quarter of all the army's motor transport), manned by nearly 9,000 officers and men, some 1,700 lorries took to the road each day. As soon as thirty lorries had been filled, a convoy was despatched, preceded by a car carrying the convoy commander. The lorries travelled in groups of five, with a small gap between groups, and any vehicle that broke down was simply pushed off the road into the ditch.

Troops normally disembarked from the train at Baudonvilliers, south-west of Bar-le-Duc. They were then carried by lorry as far as Nixéville or Blercourt, south-west of Verdun, before marching the final few kilometres to the front lines, this last leg of the journey within range of the German guns. Those heading to rest were taken to villages north-west of Bar-le-Duc, like Brabant-le-Roi, Revigny-sur-Ornain or Neuville-sur-Ornain, or south to Saint-Dizier and Ligny-en-Barrois. The whole system was likened to a 'noria', a chain of buckets continually filling and emptying, or a 'tourniquet', a turnstile constantly revolving, and allowed an average of 15,000 to 20,000 men and 2,500 tonnes of matériel and munitions to be transported to the front each day. Of the three transport groups on the Verdun front, one carried 900,000 men in seven months, the second 730,000 in five months, and the third 300,000 in two months. At Pétain's Souilly HQ, which stood at the side of the road, a lorry passed every fourteen seconds. After the war the role of this vital artery was celebrated in the name 'La Voie Sacrée'.

The wounded were taken for treatment to hospitals in the rear set up by Second Army's director of medical services, Alfred Mignon. The ex-director of the army medical school at Val-de-Grâce in Paris, Mignon had arrived at Verdun in early February 1916 to find operating theatres being used as storerooms and a complete absence of preparations to cope with an influx of wounded. He immediately set to work, attaching aid posts and ambulance units to front-line formations, sending forward mobile surgical units, auto-chirs, to perform urgent operations closer to the front line, and increasing the number of beds available. Patients at existing hospitals – typhoid cases at Les Glorieux in Verdun, the disabled at the Petit Méribel in Verdun, and others at general hospitals in Brocourt and Chaumont-sur-Aire – were evacuated to the rear, and four new hospitals were established south-west of the city at Baleycourt, Petit-Monthairons, Revigny-sur-Ornain and Bar-le-Duc, each with its own evacuation lines.

Although exposed to German artillery over its final stretch, the rest of the Voie Sacrée remained relatively unscathed throughout the battle. Despite the Germans' extensive use of airpower their bombers were used mainly in an infantry support role and bombing raids were few. Zeppelin LZ77 was shot down over Revigny-sur-Ornain in February 1916, shortly after the fighting began, but the airship was returning from a raid on Paris rather than targeting this important railway junction. On 1 June a raid on Bar-le-Duc killed some sixty people and injured many more – but the strategic damage was slight and retaliation swift. Three weeks later the French mounted a reprisal raid on Karlsruhe, killing over a hundred civilians and injuring many more.

Verdun, 25 June 1916. The men of the Verdun garrison led a troglodytic existence among the heavily shelled ruins. In the background is the Tour Saint-Vanne, the last vestige of the medieval abbey that stood within the grounds of the citadel, here being used to support a wireless mast. 'In the feeble electric light, I passed through hall after hall filled with soldiers,' reported Sous-lieutenant René Arnaud (337th Infantry). 'Some were changing their clothes after the march for fear of catching cold … others gobbling down food from their mess-tins or drinking from their water-bottles. All these casemates with their tiny, porthole-like windows and thick pillars supporting the low ceiling reminded me of the between-decks in a boat full of immigrants.'

Assigning billets was the job of the town major, pictured here in the citadel with the large blackboards displaying the current arrangements. The front-line soldier often regarded his counterparts in the rear with a jaundiced eye, but not so at Verdun. 'There are no shirkers [here],' opined Captain Louis Bourricaud (323rd Infantry). 'Everyone does his duty and this perhaps more than anything bolsters the morale of the poilus.'

Dombasle-en-Argonne, 9 March 1916. Herds of cattle requisitioned from local farmers provided fresh meat. Each army corps and army was supposed to maintain a seven-day supply of meat 'on the hoof', but careful cooking was required. 'Meat from recently slaughtered animals will not have been hung long enough to be roasted or grilled,' advised the official army manuals. 'Braising and boiling are the only ways of making sure it will be edible and palatable.' Each man had a daily ration of 500g of meat, plus 750g of bread and 100g of vegetables. As emergency rations, he also carried 300g of biscuit and 300g of corned beef.

A soldier is tasked with disinfecting street-side urinals as part of the effort to keep the citadel clean and disease free. Adjudant Lefeuvre of 65th Infantry recoiled from the conditions he found on his arrival on 11 June 1916: 'the regiment is literally crammed into some of the outbuildings in the citadel. The surroundings are disgustingly filthy: huge piles of waste stinking to high heaven; discarded meat swarming with maggots. It's a miracle that no epidemic has broken out. A poor first impression.'

Verdun, 23 July 1916. Mobile cookers operate in the ditch of the fortress. 'GQG seems to have been too busy to treat the supply of food with the same care it devoted to that of ammunition,' grumbled one soldier. '[Otherwise], they might have found something more appetizing for men in the front line than boiled rice, which goes off after a few hours. They might have bothered to taste the ration beans, sparing us from wondering why they so often smelled of wet dog. They might also have refrained from supplying heavily spiced meat and salted herring to men who were dying of thirst.'

Field Bakery 21 hard at work, Champ de Mars, Verdun, 21 November 1916. 'The citadel of Verdun is unique in the world, quite impregnable,' marvelled François Ferrec of 294th Infantry. 'No shell, whatever its calibre, could rattle a fortress built into a hillside, and it was vital to our victory in the battle. A new division was billeted there every day. That's where the bread was baked for the sector and where all kinds of rations were available; for the first time in my life I ate army bread that was fresh and warm.'

The newly baked loaves are piled high, ready to be distributed to the units. Each loaf weighed 1.5kg, equivalent to two days' bread ration for one man, and was expected to last five days in summer and eight in winter. According to a contemporary English journalist, the bakery produced 30,000 loaves a day, alone requiring up to 15 tonnes of flour.

Baleycourt, 22 June 1916. The hills on the left bank of the Meuse were very short of springs, so supplying fresh water for the front-line troops was a priority. Here, a pump from Second Army's water service fills barrels from springs 7km south-west of the city. All front-line soldiers suffered terribly from thirst, especially during the summer months: 'We soon got through the two litres we carried in our water-bottles,' reported Daniel Mornet (231st Infantry). 'We worked hard and were thirsty nearly all the time. We were often in dire need of water. There was none on the left bank. On the right bank … there were lots of springs. But the Germans knew that just as well as we did … and shelled them so heavily you risked your life every time you went for a drink.'

A water filtration wagon donated by the Touring Club de France, Dugny, 11 January 1916. Water was purified by adding 1 to 4mg of chlorine per litre, followed by sodium thiosulphate to remove the excess, making it safe – if unpleasant – to drink. 'The chlorine', noted distinguished civil engineer Philippe Bunau-Varilla, 'gave the water a dreadful taste reminiscent of the smell of the bleach used to disinfect the latrines.' In fact, a smaller dose of chlorine would also have done the trick, without the noxious side-effects.

Near Fort Moulainville, January 1916. Ration wine is transferred from large barrels into smaller ones for distribution to the regiments. 'I never suffered from thirst like I did in the Bois Fumin between 18 and 23 June,' recalled Corporal Léon Brunea (67th Infantry). 'One day the poor old territorials arrived with a two-litre water bottle full of wine and presented it to Quartermaster-Sergeant C. He started swigging from it with our Lieutenant E… . ignoring us completely. "The sods aren't going to leave us any," I muttered. [By that time] my chums and I had drunk our own urine with a bit of sugar, sucked on tree roots, swallowed the brine from a tin the Boches had left on the parapet. Eventually C. gave me a cup of wine, just the one, and even then not filled to the brim. I shared it with my chums. What a relief, even though the urine had burned our palates.'

General Pétain installed his HQ in the *mairie* at Souilly, south-west of Verdun, right beside the Voie Sacrée. The public tap in front of the building is a Wallace fountain. These fountains – designed and presented by British philanthropist Sir Richard Wallace (1818–90) to bring fresh water to the city of Paris after the destruction of the Franco-Prussian war – are still a common feature of the capital's street scene. They were later installed elsewhere in France, as well as in cities all over the world.

Accompanied by the band, machine-gun carts pass along the Voie Sacrée through Souilly as a regiment heads to rest. General Pétain often watched his men from the steps of his HQ: 'It broke my heart to see these 20-year-old boys going into the front line. I watched them with great fondness as they moved up with their units. Huddling in uncomfortable lorries, or bowed beneath the weight of their pack, they tried their best to appear unconcerned.... But how demoralized they were on their return ... the ranks of their company thinned by losses. They stared straight ahead as if transfixed by a vision of horror.'

Second Army HQ, Souilly, 14 March 1916. Joffre arrives to ginger up General Pétain. He admired the General for his 'very great military qualities', but also considered him overly cautious: 'he was too inclined, probably as a matter of temperament, to believe that the only possible strategy was a defensive one.' Six weeks later, Joffre finally lost patience with Pétain's insistent demands for fresh troops, promoting him to command Central Army Group and replacing him with General Robert Nivelle.

Refugees outside the Hôtel du Raisin Blanc, Souilly, 4 March 1916. The refugees scattered throughout France but were not always guaranteed a warm welcome. In Menton, for instance, their new neighbours accused them of being 'spies, almost German', while a child living in Spéracédès, outside Grasse, found: 'There are plenty of nice, friendly people in this village, but a lot are beastly, calling us Germans and Boches.'

Staff officers add the latest intelligence to artillery maps at RVF Headquarters, Dugny, 1 January 1916. The French first began making widespread use of aerial photography to update their maps during the September 1915 offensive in Champagne, standardizing on three scales: 1/20,000 for the artillery, 1/10,000 for the infantry and 1/5,000 for use during attacks. 'Once complete, the trench maps gave an accurate picture of the terrain and identified every target,' wrote Paul-Louis Weiller. 'The aviator and the gunner could at last jointly agree their objectives ... Commanders could see the whole of the enemy defences and evaluate their strengths and weaknesses. In short, they obtained a clear picture of everything lying in front of them.'

RFV Headquarters, Dugny, 9.00pm, 1 January 1916. The NCOs of the RFV see in the New Year in convivial fashion in their mess. The man opening the bottle of champagne (seated, second right) is a member of the permanent corps of staff clerks. His companions are drawn from a variety of different units and include a naval petty officer (seated, first right). The Dugny HQ was housed in a building owned by Senator Charles Humbert, a member of the senate committee of enquiry in September 1915.

Brocourt-en-Argonne, May 1916. North African troops of 45th Division pass through this left-bank village en route to their pick-up in Nixéville, leaving behind hard fighting around Côte 304 and Avocourt.

Nixéville, 8 April 1916. Weapons piled, men wait to be picked up by lorry after coming out of the lines around Fort Vaux. The final stage of the journey to and from the front lines, within range of the German guns, was a perilous one. On 1 June 1916 a company of 150 men from II/75th Infantry left Bévaux Barracks (the former cavalry barracks on the east side of Verdun): 'we reached the front line with just thirty men left, and that was before we'd even encountered the enemy.'

Near Heippes, 7 March 1916. Territorials wait by the roadside while Renault lorries pass in convoy along the Voie Sacrée. The two crewmen in the vehicle nearest the camera are wrapped in heavy fur coats – a common, if unofficial, choice for drivers in these open cabs, who spent 'night after night riveted to the wheel, exhausted, stiff from lack of movement, grabbing a bite to eat from a hand swollen with frostbite [and] slathered in frozen Vaseline … struggling against the cold, battling in particular the relentless, cruel tyranny of sleep … lulled into a trance by the constant thrum of the engine.'

Near Heippes, 7 March 1916. Lorries of transport unit TM222 carry North African troops to the battle. In the snow and ice of February 1916, at the height of the initial German assault, the lorries of TM388 travelled 685km in four days, ferrying 146th and 206th Infantry to Verdun, and evacuating the battle-weary men of the 127th and 206th. 'I've never been so hungry or cold in my life,' sighed one of the drivers.

Near Regret, 8 April 1916. The men of 332nd Infantry (69th Division) disembark from the lorries of TM362, which will immediately pick up the waiting 201st Infantry (1st Division). The 332nd was bound for Mort-Homme, where it would stay until 3 June. The men of the 201st had been in the lines around Bras and the Côte de Poivre since 29 February; they were taken by lorry to Saint Dizier and then by train to Dormans, on the Marne. 'Without the lorries of the Voie Sacrée, Verdun would eventually have capitulated,' affirmed Pétain in 1929.

Route de Rampont, near Vadelaincourt, May 1916. A machine-gun section moves to the rear, passing an artillery battery heading the other way. Every section had two of the small carts seen here, each capable of carrying one machine gun and six boxes of ammunition. Every infantry regiment included three machine-gun companies, each composed of three or four of these sections.

Souilly, 13 March 1916. The men of 409th Infantry (120th Division) head to the rear. In five days of hard fighting around the Ouvrage d'Hardaumont, north of Fort Vaux, the regiment had lost 1,500 men. One man (centre) is wearing a German shako taken as a souvenir. At Érize-la-Grande, south of Souilly, Sous-lieutenant René Arnaud and his men (337th Infantry) watched as other troops returned from the line, 'faces as grey as their greatcoats, covered in ten days' growth of beard. Some were wearing trophies seized from the Germans, filthy grey helmets and forage caps. Legs dangling from the tailboards, they seemed to regard us with a hostile air, as if to say, "Now it's your turn."'

Vadelaincourt, 25 May 1916. Loading Ariès 4-tonne lorries with stones intended for road repairs. Ten cubic metres of stone were used every day. To the routine damage caused by traffic and weather was added that inflicted by bombs and shells. 'If a shell or a bomb from a plane landed on the road and left a crater, the nearest team of territorials rushed to repair it,' recalled Louis Lefebvre (78th Infantry). 'There were plenty of incidents but they didn't interrupt things for long. Each man knew his duty and hastened to perform it, however dangerous it might be.'

Territorials of the road repair squads are handed their duties, Rampont. 'The road must hold at all costs,' ordered GQG in February 1916, and its maintenance was vital to eventual victory. Quarries were opened in villages along the route to extract the soft limestone of the region, and work went on around the clock, most urgently during the sudden thaw at the end of that month. The constant flow of traffic made it impossible to use steamrollers to consolidate the surface. The lorries themselves did the job, while territorials armed with picks and shovels threw new stones on the road between the passage of the convoys.

Bar-le-Duc, 1 June 1916. At 12.45pm on 1 June two waves of enemy bombers struck Bar-le-Duc, at the southern end of the *Meusien* line and the Voie Sacrée. The townsfolk had just finished their midday meal when the roar of engines sounded in the skies above. People left their houses to watch 'as if it were an air display' and casualties were high, with some sixty civilians dead and many injured. Only two days later the victims were honoured in an elaborate funeral attended by the wife of President Raymond Poincaré. Then on 22 June the French had their revenge: a reprisal raid on Karlsruhe hit a circus performance in the town's former station, killing over a hundred and injuring many more.

Supply vehicles wait to load from railway wagons, Bar-le-Duc, 11 March 1916. The town's importance to the supply effort is amply demonstrated in this crowded scene. Driver Joseph Vidal was part of a convoy that departed on 5 March 1916: 'the officers left their lorries and men exposed to potential enemy fire for six to twelve hours,' he grumbled. 'They did nothing to make the day any less dangerous or difficult for the majority of them. About fifty lorries left Triaucourt at 5.30am to transport matériel from Bar-le-Duc station to one of the Verdun forts. They could only be loaded ten at a time at Bar-le-Duc, then unloaded singly at Verdun. After waiting three hours to be loaded, the lorries then remained at the fort from 2.00pm to 1.00am waiting to be unloaded. They could have left Triaucourt two and a half hours later, and waited in the village for unloading, less exposed to the cold and shells, with no harm at all to the service.'

Camp de la Madeleine, near Fort Moulainville, January 1916. Transport wagons assemble on a dreary winter's day. Once matériel had been delivered in bulk to the depots in Regret or Dugny, further distribution was the responsibility of divisional and regimental transport, nearly all of it horse-drawn.

Dombasle-en-Argonne, 17 March 1916. Fresh ammunition is distributed from this depot, which serviced artillery units on the left bank. Prior to the outbreak of war, the French estimated that they would need 13,600 rounds of 75mm ammunition a day; by the summer of 1916 they were using 77,000 a day, plus 24,000 heavy shells. 'Ever longer ranges, ever larger calibres, ever faster rates of fire, ever more guns in the line,' commented General Herr. 'These are the lessons of Verdun.'

Dombasle-en-Argonne, 20 March 1916. Spent shell cases were collected in huge numbers. 'Relieved tonight,' reported one soldier. 'We halted in the Forêt de Hesse, and again in the Bois de Béthelainville. In the darkness we passed a heap of 75mm shell cases. It was 500m long, a mere nothing!'

Bar-le-Duc, 3 April 1916. Troops head to the front on the trains of *Le Meusien*. This metre-gauge line opened in 1887–8 and closed in 1936. In peacetime the journey between Bar-le-Duc and Verdun took 2¼ hours. Although the *Meusien* line carried some troops, its primary role was to transport rations to Verdun and evacuate the wounded on its return.

Bar-le-Duc, 2 April 1916. The men enjoying a final cup of coffee outside the station are a mixed bunch from several different regiments – infantry, territorial infantry and chasseurs alpins. Ironically, the army had opposed the building of the *Meusien* line, fearing it could be used by an invading enemy.

Laying track for the new standard-gauge railway line, 6bis. Work began in February, and the Dugny and Clermont lines were open by late June. However, despite the best efforts of ten battalions of territorials, plus Algerian, Indochinese and Malagasy labourers, as well as German prisoners, problems bridging the river Aire delayed completion of a second spur to Dombasle-en-Argonne until 25 September.

The ammunition depot at Maison Rouge, near Fort Regret, June 1916. German prisoners are hard at work on a new narrow-gauge railway line designed to extend the *Meusien* network with extra spurs leading to depots behind the front line.

Near Froidos, May 1916. Men relax behind the lines, some 30km south-west of Verdun, taking the opportunity to enjoy the warmer weather and wash themselves and their clothes. 'That's two nights we've spent in this underground shelter,' complained François Mauris (403rd Infantry). 'The lice are devouring us; they breed with a terrifying fecundity; born in the morning, grandparents by evening.'

Men bathe in the Meuse near the La Falouse quarries, Belleray, July 1916. The small redoubt at La Falouse, 8km south of Verdun, never came under fire, and the quarries served as a depot and rest area. After seeing action at the Batterie de Damloup in July 1916, Captain George Gallois (221st Infantry) was at rest near Bar-le-Duc: 'I was mentally drained, a big beard, a filthy, muddy greatcoat … stiff legs, a dislocated knee … but a good wash and two days lying on a palliasse have helped to restore my spirits … And today, like everyone else, I'm fine … completely at ease since we're out of hearing of the guns.'

Mealtime at a chasseurs alpins bivouac, La Falouse, 4 October 1916. In July 1915 the distinctive beret of the chasseurs alpins replaced the képi as a general issue forage cap for the rest of the army. However, the chasseurs had no wish to see *their* cap worn by all and sundry; they fought the move tooth and nail – and carried the day. Only six weeks later the measure was withdrawn and the beret replaced in non-alpine units by a fore-and-aft cap.

The theatre of the 44th Territorials, Dugny, 11 January 1916. The 44th was a local regiment, serving in the front line on the first night of the battle. Detachments also served at Fort Vaux and Fort Tavannes before the regiment was eventually redeployed to the Voie Sacrée. Its most famous member was local politician Sergeant André Maginot (1877–1932). Maginot was severely wounded in action in 1914, and as minister of war from 1922 he lobbied hard for a new line of fortifications to protect Alsace and Lorraine from future invasion. However, he died of typhoid fever before it was complete, and the line that eventually bore his name was largely the work of his successor, Paul Painlevé.

A group of wounded await evacuation, Fort Tavannes, 15 June 1916. Casualties were collected from the battlefield, then taken to a regimental aid post set up in a suitably sheltered spot. Each man had a card attached to his clothing, detailing his wounds and any medication already administered. Standing in the doorway, hands in pockets, is a member of the medical personnel. Sergeant Jean Lou de las Borjas (7th Infantry) described his experience of Casemate B at Fort Souville: 'It was a vaulted shelter constructed from solid stone and covered with a layer of earth 5m or 6m thick. The severely wounded had been waiting here for over six days for transport to a medical unit. Some were in absolute agony. They'd had nothing to eat and were in dreadful pain from their ruined limbs. All would die one after another. It was painful to see these brave men and hear their cries for help; but there was nothing we could do for them except give them something to eat and, most of all, to drink.'

Lines of Communication Hospital No. 6, La Queue de Mala, near Vadelaincourt, 27 June 1916. The wounded were taken from the aid posts to a field hospital to be triaged. 'Have you ever been to Vadelaincourt?' asked one British ambulance driver. 'Of course not. Well, don't go! It is a little village 15 kilometres from Verdun, and lies at the bottom of a muddy little valley with a muddy little stream running through it. In fine weather it is all dust; in wet, thick soupy mud.' Here, a British Red Cross ambulance, donated by the Northumberland and Durham Coal Owners, unloads its cargo of wounded. Each ambulance could carry five stretcher cases, or eight to twelve seated patients.

The volunteer drivers of American ambulance unit SSU5, Dugny, 16 August 1916. SSU5, also known as the Norton-Harjes Ambulance, recruited its members among alumni of Harvard University. 'Since arriving [we] have had strenuous times,' wrote unit commander Richard Norton. 'We are camped some five miles outside Verdun, where we have our permanent post; another is at a hospital between us and Verdun; while every night, as soon as it is dark, we send out eight cars to evacuate the advanced posts. This is extremely risky work and can only be done at night, owing to the road being in view of the Germans, who are not a kilometre distant.'

The volunteer drivers of SSA18, a British Red Cross ambulance unit, Dugny, 17 October 1916. 'At eleven we have *dejeuner* or "soupe",' recalled a driver from SSA10. 'There is a long, cranky table down the centre of the tent, and cranky forms unevenly balanced on which to sit. The cook (who isn't a cook, as alas! we found out long ago, but a barber in Paris) brings in some hot meat and vegetables. These last are generally white beans; there seems to be a scarcity of potatoes. The meat may or may not be eatable, the odds are against it, but there are parcels from England. Perhaps someone has brought out a ham – its life is short – and there are tinned peaches and apricots and jam, with bread and butter. The latter, happily generally tastes better than it smells… . No, on the whole, we don't live luxuriously.'

Dugny, 17 October 1916. This ambulance from SSA18, a gift of the Derbyshire and Nottinghamshire Coal Owners, is in need of repair after being hit by a shell while evacuating casualties around Fort Souville. The vehicles of SSA10 were luckier: 'So far not even a car has been seriously hit, though it is rather marvellous how they escaped,' reported William Leng. 'Mine, with myself in it, was in the outside zone of a shrapnel the other day. Bullets splashed all round, digging up the earth, but not a touch on the car. Do the shrapnel recognize that we are non-combatants and are only there to succour the wounded?'

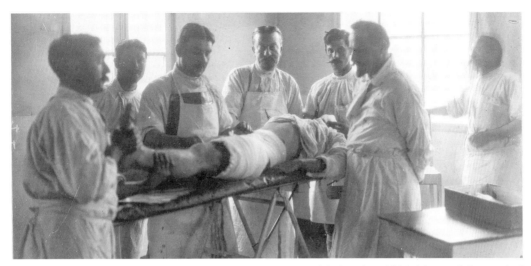

Operating theatre, Military Hospital No. 12, Vadelaincourt, 24 October 1916. None of the surgical team is wearing a mask, but a government minister was full of admiration for their 'knowledge, ingenuity and hard work … protecting our troops from infection, healing their wounds, mending their fractures, producing men fit for military service or citizens able … to resume a trade'. Nurses, too, were praised: 'nothing deterred them … neither the dreadful wounds nor their humble tasks'.

Lines of Communication Hospital No. 20, Bar-le-Duc, 2 April 1916. Inside the Salle Lerey, a ward for lightly wounded men. 'A wound!' thought René Naegelen, marching into the front line. 'This magical word rings in our ears. A wound, a good wound. Every man nurtures this hope deep down!' In the first week of the German offensive the hospital dealt with 6,578 cases. 'Good soldiers that they are, the wounded say little,' commented one man. 'Not because they're overwhelmed by pain but because so many images are running through their mind – images of combat, of extreme tiredness, of blood and mud, images of past and future, of going home – but as an invalid. [Yesterday's] home may tomorrow be in mourning.'

Bar-le-Duc, 12 March 1916. Stretcher cases are loaded aboard a train for evacuation to hospitals across France. 'Then after hospital, convalescence!' wrote Henri Surle (58th Territorials). 'How wonderful to be back in nice clean clothes! But my [biggest] surprise came when I was taken into the mess hall and found a plate, cutlery and napkin at my place; I burst into tears, scarcely able to believe my eyes.'

Souilly, 19 December 1916. Mealtime at a temporary pen used as a holding area for prisoners of war until they could be moved to permanent camps in the interior. The temporary pens were normally run by provost detachments, and Souilly was the alleged scene of summary executions and other mistreatment. The majority of permanent camps were located in *départements* on the Atlantic seaboard, although some 6,000 men were sent to Morocco. The prisoners were employed in agriculture or public works – repairing roads or railways, for example – and were normally guarded by local territorial units. 'Most prisoners of war are satisfied with their treatment,' stated the Red Cross in 1918, reporting on camps in the Meuse *département*. 'They say that their previous food and accommodation were very poor.' However, Helmut Korth (Bay.IR 47), who transited through Souilly after his capture at Verdun in November 1916, would beg to differ: he entitled his account of his time in French prison camps *Wir weißen Sklaven* (*We White Slaves*).

Chapter Four

We are Gaining the Upper Hand

Throughout March and April 1916 Pétain and Joffre found themselves increasingly at odds. Pétain later claimed that 'GQG failed to appreciate all the problems we faced'; meanwhile Joffre, with one eye on his forthcoming Somme offensive, was exasperated beyond measure by Pétain's repeated demands for more men and guns. 'You are aware of the general strategic situation,' he informed his stubborn commander on 2 April. 'You should therefore do everything in your power to ensure I am not forced to deploy the last fresh corps at my disposal.' Joffre was also frustrated by Pétain's innate caution. To the Intelligence Section, it was the Germans who were now under pressure: they had failed to achieve their original objectives, casualties were mounting and morale was starting to falter. The time was ripe for the French to adopt a more aggressive strategy.

On 1 May Joffre confirmed the change by kicking Pétain upstairs to command Central Army Group, with the current commander of III Corps, the belligerent Robert Nivelle, taking over Second Army. 'It was with a profound sense of sadness that I relinquished control of Second Army to General Nivelle,' recalled Pétain. 'I set up my new headquarters at Bar-le-Duc and prepared to do my utmost to execute the commander-in-chief's orders, "to retain all the positions currently held on Central Army Group's front and ... to recapture Fort Douaumont". To this end I had twenty-four divisions, maintained solely from the resources of Central Army Group. I was even expected to try to manage with fewer.'

A simple artillery colonel in August 1914, Nivelle had enjoyed a rapid rise through brigade, divisional and corps command. On 6 May he expounded his philosophy of battle in a letter to his corps commanders : 'Recent experience in the Verdun sector has proven the superiority in every respect of aggressive over wholly passive defence. Losses within a given formation have been fewer during partial offensives than during periods of completely passive defence. The explanation is simple: if we do not attack, the enemy will, and the attacker takes prisoners whose number can be added to losses inflicted by fire... . The attacker [also] puts himself in a position to capture trenches and prisoners, rather than lose them to the enemy, and to systematically straighten his lines as a basis for future attacks. In addition, the morale of troops employed in an attacking role improves beyond the most optimistic of expectations, while those stuck on the defensive inevitably become demoralized, and often dangerously so... . The commander of Second Army commends these tactics, so productive on the ground and in terms of morale, to any formation commander yet to adopt them. Their impact will serve only to confirm the conviction we share, and are obliged to convey to all, that we are gradually gaining the upper hand.'

For all Nivelle's fine words, the Germans were not finished yet. On the left bank, seventy-five enemy batteries concentrated their fire on Côte 304 on 3 May, but the positions of 68th Infantry remained largely intact and the attack was repulsed. So, too, were further attacks over three successive days from 5–7 June. In an attempt to flank the position, the Germans managed to capture the village of Avocourt, but Côte 304 remained in French hands. On Mort-Homme a German gas attack on 20 June succeeded in infiltrating the positions of 296th Infantry, but again the French rallied and drove the enemy back.

On the right bank Nivelle launched an attack on Fort Douaumont, a target whose recapture had hypnotized French commanders, transcending simple battlefield advantage to become a matter of national prestige. With its 155mm and 75mm gun-turrets both out of action, the Germans were using the captured fort as a shelter. The French bombarded it with large-calibre shells, including 400s fired from naval guns, and attempted several unsuccessful assaults. Then on 8 May came an accidental explosion in a grenade store, which killed some 800 German soldiers. After a ferocious artillery duel on 20 May, the French attacked again two days later and managed to gain a toehold on the fort's ruined superstructure. However, their position was untenable and they were quickly driven off, with heavy casualties on both sides.

The Germans now turned their attention to the neighbouring Fort Vaux, resuming their attacks on 28 May. The four redoubts guarding the left flank of the fort (R1 to R4) were reduced one by one, and the supporting infantry killed, captured or forced to withdraw. Inside the fort, Major Raynal and his 500 men fought on – deprived of support on their flanks, isolated by German artillery fire, short of rations, dazed by the dust, fumes and constant explosions, but confident in the supply of fresh water from their 5,000l cistern. Then, to his horror, Raynal discovered that the cistern was cracked and most of its contents had drained away. 'I tour our posts,' he wrote. 'Exhaustion is etched on every face, my words no longer serve to rouse them … My words of encouragement produce no reaction; any man who looks me in the eye does so with a dazed expression. They are suffering and I believe they can endure no more.' A French relief effort failed, and on 7 June, after three days without water, Raynal surrendered.

Buoyed by this success, the Germans launched an attempt on the inner line of right-bank fortifications, south of Fort Douaumont and Fort Vaux, ushering in a period of intense struggle over the intervening ground. The Ouvrage de Froideterre, guarding the western extremity of the Douaumont ridge, remained in French hands throughout, but positions in and around the Ouvrage de Thiaumont, the village of Fleury, the Bois Fumin and Bois Laufée were the focus of fierce fighting over the next two months. On 22 June, after a day of intensive bombardment, the enemy infantry made progress towards Fort Souville, using the new phosgene gas and novel infiltration tactics to capture the Ouvrage de Thiaumont and the French position in Fleury. For days the struggle raged around Thiaumont, the position swapping hands several times until the Germans finally took possession on 4 July. Meanwhile, south of Fort Vaux, the Germans entered the Batterie de Damloup on the heels of a violent bombardment, but a rump of some twenty men from a French infantry company held out until nightfall, when reinforcements arrived to force the enemy out.

By now, though, the Germans were running out of men. Troops were required to shore up the eastern front after the success of the Brusilov offensive, and the opening of the Anglo-

French offensive on the Somme on 1 July was a further drain on the enemy reserves. To some German commanders, every success at Verdun seemed to demand yet another attack to secure previous gains, and the Crown Prince was increasingly reluctant to commit the men necessary. In a last desperate bid to capture all the heights, Falkenhayn authorized a limited offensive targeting Fort Souville. On 12 July the Germans reached the ditch of the fort, but French counter-attacks drove them back before they could penetrate further.

General Robert Nivelle, Second Army HQ, Souilly, 9 November 1916. 'Touchy, pushy, a military dilettante', sniffed General Hubert Lyautey, briefly minister of war in 1917. Yet Joffre responded warmly to his new man's positive outlook. 'Nivelle was the chief architect [of our victory at Verdun],' stated the commander-in-chief. 'While his senior officer [Pétain] was despatching bleak reports to the minister of war, he displayed a rare ability to rise above the battlefield, understand his role in my overall strategy, and retain his composure and will to win.' Having replaced Pétain as commander of Second Army, Nivelle went on to oust Joffre himself in December 1916, vowing to repeat his success at Verdun on a broader front. But only five months later he too was sacked – his reputation destroyed by the abject failure of his Chemin des Dames offensive – and replaced in his turn by Pétain.

Côte 304, 5 May 1916. The German bombardment of this key left-bank position is viewed from a French reconnaissance aircraft from MF33, the trench lines clearly visible. 'It was no longer a bombardment but a cyclone of fire,' recalled the regimental history of 114th Infantry. 'The Boches have just launched an attack on Côte 304 and Mort-Homme,' wrote Lieutenant Charles Armeilla (20th Artillery). 'Never have I seen such an avalanche of shells; the smoke rose to an incredible height, forming a barrier so thick that the sun was unable to penetrate it.' By the time the battle was over, the hill was 7 metres lower in height.

German soldiers fetch water from a shell-hole on Côte 304. Sous-lieutenant Louis Campana (151st Infantry) watched one of his own men reduced to a similar extremity: '[he was] taking big gulps from a pond covered in green scum. It contained a body floating on its stomach, bloated as if it had been taking in water for days.'

Bois d'Esnes, south of Côte 304, 1916. Men from 84th Heavy Artillery use a tramway to bring up shells for the batteries located in the wood. Formed in November 1915, with some batteries joining as recently as January 1916, the regiment was a relatively new creation. It was equipped with a mixture of 100TR, 120L and 155L guns.

Soldiers take a nap in the reserve trenches, Fort Bois Bourrus, 16 June 1916. The fort was completed in 1886 and remained behind French lines throughout the battle. Although heavily bombarded by 105mm and 150mm shells from February onwards, damage was restricted to the outer masonry. The main reinforced concrete structure could only be penetrated by the larger calibre 210s and 380s, which fortunately were rare. Life in the reserve trenches brought precious little chance to rest. 'From 1 June to 5 June we entered the lines each night,' remembered one poilu from 71st Infantry. 'It was no picnic making our way along more or less obliterated communications trenches, under constant shelling, to repair the front-line trenches damaged in the earlier fighting. About 6km of communications trenches separated the Bois Le Bouchet from the front lines, snaking through the Bois Bourrus.'

Rue des Fontaines, Montzéville, 25 July 1916. A couple of soldiers seize a quiet moment to do their laundry at the public tap, still visible today, in this village behind the French lines south of Mort-Homme.

Fort de Marre, May 1916. An aerial view taken by a reconnaissance plane from MF33. Fort de Marre was one of the original Verdun forts, lying on the left bank of the Meuse, between Fort Bois Bourrus and Fort Vacherauville, with long views down the valley and across the river to the Côte de Talou. Some 6,000 shells landed on the fort between April and October 1916, but again the main works remained unscathed. None of the Verdun defences was out of range of the German guns, which could reach as far as Nixéville, some 12km south of the city.

Preparing barbed-wire entanglements in the Avocourt sector, April 1916. Lying at the foot of the heights dominated by Côte 304, the village of Avocourt was progressively strengthened by the French as the Germans broadened their attacks on the left bank in March and April. Its fall in early June marked the western culmination of German incursions into French positions.

Avocourt, April 1916. A soldier consults his map while his lucky comrade grabs the opportunity for forty winks. 'It's impossible to snatch a moment's rest,' wrote Charles Delvert (101st Infantry) in the trenches around Fort Vaux in early June. 'I haven't slept for almost seventy-two hours.'

Avocourt, July 1916. Rifle resting rather casually against the trench wall, a sentry stands guard in the lines outside the village. A niche in the wall contains a grenade for emergencies. 'There aren't many troops in the first line of trenches,' explained Daniel Mornet (278th Infantry). 'They are there as sentries to foil a surprise attack, not to break up a major assault.'

A 58mm T1bis trench mortar, Avocourt defences, July 1916. Despite its short range and small explosive charge, this mortar remained in service until 1918. On the broken ground of the Verdun battlefield, it was hard to set up and to carry the heavy bombs required. Infantrymen were always sceptical of trench mortars. The gunners would arrive and position them in the front line, fire a few rounds, then disappear. When the inevitable retribution arrived, 'it was always the infantrymen who paid for any breakages'.

The Ferme de la Tuilerie, near Thierville, 25 June 1916. A 155mm gun belonging to 9th Battery, 5th Group, 85th Heavy Artillery, fires a night-time mission from its position at the farm, which lay directly across the river from Verdun.

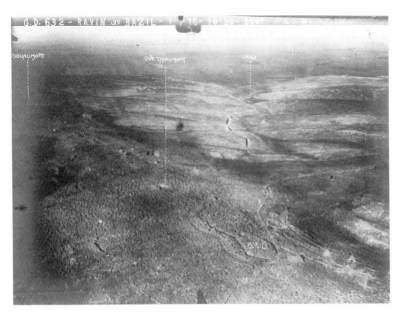

Looking east down the Ravin du Bazil, 1 July 1916. In this aerial view, taken from 800m above the battlefield by a machine from MF33, Fort Douaumont is on the left, the Ouvrage de Thiaumont in the centre, and the village of Vaux on the right. Fort Vaux is just visible on the crest of the ridge to the right.

The entrance to Fort Vaux, 11 March 1916. 'Eight thousand shells a day landed on the fort and its surrounds and that was on a quiet day,' recalled Corporal Lucien Laurent (7/51 Engineers Company), who spent a fortnight inside the fort between 2 and 17 May 1916. 'We existed in utter squalor, with a fortnight's growth of beard, covered in lice, amid the pungent stench of blood from the infirmary, simply a casemate full of the wounded, where the dead lay waiting for nightfall when we could throw them in the ditch. We squelched through urine in the latrines, the smell of ammonia making the air unbreathable. Men crowded every corridor, a jumble of bodies lying wherever they could. We were all so tired that we only had to sit or lie down for a few seconds to fall asleep immediately.'

A command post established at the Petit Dépôt, Fort Vaux, June 1916. The depot acted as a reserve ammunition magazine, some distance from the fort, and separate from the fort's own reserves.

Bois de la Vaux-Régnier, 16 July 1916. From his location in the wood, an officer takes up his binoculars to observe the German positions opposite. By the spring of 1916, the 'wood' was devoid of trees – just a bare hillside rising gently towards Fort Vaux.

An officer peers from an infantry HQ dug-out, Bois de Vaux-Chapitre, 20 June 1916. The wood lay on the hillside south of Vaux village, on the left flank of Fort Vaux, overlooking the Ravin du Bazil. 'I almost forgot to tell you about the Bois de Vaux-Chapitre, even though it's mentioned in the communiqués,' Jean Bousquet (206th Infantry) wrote to his parents. 'It's in front of our company and to our left, in contact with the battalion from the 344th. There were still a few stumps and tree trunks when we got here; two days later all had been flattened, roots shooting into the air with every shell. All that was left were overlapping craters, a handful of tree trunks, big shrapnel shells exploding overhead with massive force.'

A shelter in the Bois Fumin, 27 July 1916. The Bois Fumin was the section of the Bois de Vaux-Chapitre closest to Fort Vaux and the scene of fierce fighting in the early summer of 1916. When the enemy attacked on 23 June 1916, 67th Infantry lost one-third of its strength in defending the position. In July the Germans returned in force as part of their final attack on Fort Souville.

A cramped trench in the Bois Fumin, 23 July 1916. 'Many French trenches [at Verdun] were simple saps with very rough firing steps,' recalled Jacques Péricard (95th Infantry), later a spokesman for ex-combatants and compiler of an oral history of the battle. 'The support trenches behind were few and not very deep. Dug-outs were equally rare and lacked any kind of amenity: water ran everywhere, pooling on the ground; there were no benches to sit on, not even a nail from which to hang your haversack and water-bottle. A correspondent of mine who fought on Mort-Homme says that his dug-out had no illuminating rockets, the dozen coloured rockets had no sticks and four of the remaining eight had no primer. Lack of planning from above and apathy from below would again cost us dear.'

A machine-gun post in the Bois Fumin, 23 July 1916. In the distance is Fort Douaumont. Captain Charles Delvert (101st Infantry) described his position in the wood during the German assault on Fort Vaux on 1 June: 'The ouvrage is a high talus overlooking a shelled communications trench, now a line of craters. On the parados and in the trench lie stiff corpses, each covered with a tent section. Everywhere, left and right, the ground is littered with debris: tins of food, packs ripped open, helmets with holes in them, shattered rifles.'

Ouvrage de Laufée, May 1916. The ouvrage formed part of the eastern line of the Verdun defences, lying between Fort Vaux and Fort Tavannes. The inscription above the entrance is part of a motto emblazoned on several of the forts – 'S'ensevelir sous les ruines du fort plutôt que de se rendre' [Lie buried beneath the ruined fort rather than surrender] – the words spoken by Admiral Villaret to inspire the troops defending Martinique in 1809. Despite heavy enemy bombardment and a number of attacks, Laufée remained in French hands throughout the battle, its two 75s playing an important role in harassing German troop movements around Fort Vaux.

Ouvrage de Thiaumont from the air, looking north-east, 31 May 1916. The ouvrage itself is the circular feature near the top of the picture, while left and below are the trenches of the Batterie C and Batterie B positions, and to the right the small circle of the Abri Wagner. The constant pounding of the shells gradually obliterated all landmarks and it was not unusual for men to get lost. 'On 14 June we relieved 93rd Infantry north-west of the Ferme de Thiaumont,' recalled Louis Louvart (65th Infantry). 'Two days later we came across some lads from the 93rd in our trench. They had no idea that their regiment had been relieved.' Meanwhile a padre serving with 98th Infantry had an even luckier escape. Stumbling across a soldier fast asleep in a shell-hole, he tried to rouse him. Time to move, the enemy was close! The soldier woke with a start, swearing loudly and sending the padre into a hasty retreat. All the oaths were in German!

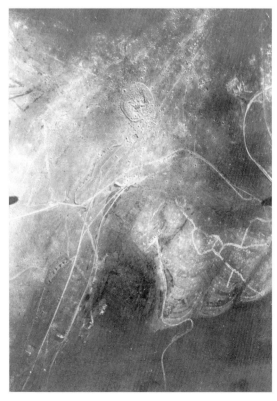

The entrance to the Abri Wagner, 24 December 1916. One of a line of three *abris de combat* built in 1908–9 to link the Ouvrage de Thiaumont to Fort Douaumont, Abri Wagner was officially known to the French as Abri TD1 (and to the Germans as Infanteriewerk 361). It could accommodate around a hundred men and its site is now part of the Douaumont Ossuary, the main French memorial at Verdun.

French soldiers try to make the best use of cover near the Ouvrage de Thiaumont, July 1916. 'Crater by crater, we reached the front lines about 200m from the Ouvrage de Thiaumont,' recalled Lieutenant Charles Henry (48th Infantry). 'The morning was quiet: no shells, nothing stirred. We knew we were going to attack, so this was the calm before the storm. At 4.00pm the bombardment began, shelling the ouvrage we were due to capture in two hours' time. The enemy didn't take long to reply and a hail of shells soon began falling around us. Several of my men were wounded, buried by a 210. Bodies exhumed by the shells gave off a foul stink. With the chorus of explosions, the whistle of the 75s and the screech of the large-calibre shells, our poor heads felt ready to burst. And still there were new victims crying for help. But zero hour was approaching. Over thirty minutes away … twenty … ten … the hand of my watch moved round implacably. Eyes glued to the dial, I counted down … my pocket crammed with rounds, my hand grasping a dead man's rifle. Slowly, I rose to my knees … 17.58 … 17.59 … 18.00 … Just as I opened my mouth to shout 'Forward', I was knocked to the ground in a blinding flash of red. I'd been shot clean through my right knee. I was also wounded in the stomach and cheek. Nearby other men were wounded, some dead …'

German soldiers desert their lines, 1 May 1916. The decision to surrender was always a dangerous moment. 'The Germans in the front line threw down their weapons [and] raised their arms shouting, "Kameraden"', reported Lucien Gissinger (174th Infantry) after a counter-attack around Douaumont village on 23 February 1916. 'Our men took no pity on them, shooting them on the spot because we had orders to take no prisoners.'

The main entrance, Fort Souville, July 1916. Fort Souville was built in 1875, one of the second line of right-bank forts. Its detached 155mm gun-turret fired some 600 shells in the first three weeks of the battle, but by 16 March 1916 the turret no longer revolved, and, with no other long-range artillery, Souville was left defenceless. After the loss of Fort Douaumont in late February, the fort was of vital strategic importance and suffered intense bombardment between May and July. The Germans briefly established a toehold here during their attack of 12 July – the closest they would come to Verdun – but were quickly driven out again.

Fort Souville, July 1916. Men from the garrison, including gunners from 50th Artillery, use a signalling lamp to request supporting fire. The fort was held by some fifty men from 7th Infantry, under Lieutenant Kléber Dupuy, alongside a handful of territorials. 'It's complete havoc here,' reported Dupuy, following his arrival on 11 July 1916. 'The commander has been gassed; the garrison is hors de combat. Until I receive a counter-order, I will remain in the fort and organize its defence.'

The remains of a 75mm gun caught in the open near the Batterie de l'Hôpital, an artillery position between Fort Souville and Fort Tavannes, July 1916. The contemporary caption notes that twelve pieces were destroyed in this small area alone. 'Batteries of 75s or 155Cs fired non-stop behind the shallowest slope or the tiniest copse, sometimes until the pieces exploded, with no shelter other than the gun itself,' recalled Gaston Lefebvre (73rd Infantry). 'Our gunners endured a hellish bombardment. Their sacrifice was just as great as our own.'

The Tavannes tunnel, western end, August 1917. The tunnel, close to Fort Tavannes, carried the main railway line east from Verdun to Étain and Metz. The line had been cut by the German advance, but the tunnel continued in use as a shelter and field hospital despite the lack of facilities. Louis Hourticq (65th Infantry) arrived there in July: 'The traffic is heavy all day, and even more so all night: water parties, ammunition parties, rations parties; troops going up, others coming down, stretcher cases brought from the battle and then evacuated. Our underground existence and the alternating spells of sleeping and waking that punctuate our lives erase any difference between night and day. The levels of activity, movement and noise are identical – continual, endless, without pause from midday to midnight, from midnight to midday. Too many people and too many things are seeking shelter inside this indestructible vault: stores of water, grenades, rockets, small-arms ammunition, explosives. Surgeons repair torn flesh under lamps black with flies. The rapid thrum of the electric generator drowns out all sound. This overheated artery seems to throb with fever.' At 9.00pm on 4 September 1916 an explosion in the ammunition stores resulted in a fire that burned for two days, killing an estimated 500 to 600 men.

Fort Tavannes, 15 June 1916. Built in 1874, Tavannes was the oldest of the Verdun forts, and is pictured here after the accidental explosion of a hand-grenade on 7 May 1916 had destroyed a powder magazine with great loss of life. Although the fort was shelled during the initial German offensive in February, it was never directly threatened by infantry attack and was used as a temporary shelter. Its official capacity was 580 men, but at one stage it held over twice that number, drawn from a dozen different regiments. The sanitary conditions were so bad that access thereafter was strictly controlled.

Boyau d'Altkirch, June 1916. A soldier picks his perilous way down this key communications trench which ran from Fort Tavannes, over the ridge, and past Fort Vaux as far as redoubt R1. It was regularly shelled by the Germans during the day and just as regularly repaired by the French overnight.

Ouvrage de Froideterre, June 1916. The ouvrage was an infantry position at the western end of the Douaumont–Thiaumont ridge, originally built in 1887–8 but completely modernized in 1902–5. After two days of enemy shelling from 21 to 23 June, debris jammed both machine-gun turrets. Yet the 75mm turret continued to fire, delivering 116 rounds at point-blank range to help drive off the German attack. Although the ouvrage came under bombardment again, it was never seriously threatened with capture.

The entrance to the Ouvrage de Froideterre, 23 May 1917. The barracks, built to hold about 140 men, are on the right; during the battle some 200 men crowded in here. Note the two machine guns mounted on poles as anti-aircraft defence.

Men wash in a shell-hole near the Ouvrage de Froideterre, June 1916. Water was too precious to spare. *L'Écho des Marmites*, the newspaper of 309th Infantry, summed up the 'highlights' of a spell in the trenches at Verdun: 'Not washing at all for a fortnight, not changing your clothes or shaving for five weeks … spending a night on sentry duty beside a cow dead for ten to fifteen days … being grazed by a shell that lands at your feet but doesn't go off … sleeping in the snow for eighteen days covered only with branches … watching your best friends die around you.'

Abri des Quatre Cheminées, 23 October 1916. The *abri*, named after its four prominent ventilation chimneys, was one of the four *abris cavernes* or large-scale shelters in the Verdun sector. It consisted of a vaulted gallery 60m long, dug 12m deep into a hillside south of the Ouvrage de Froideterre. Here, a group of colonial regimental pioneers, identifiable by their crossed-axe badge, gather outside the entrance. The position came under attack from flame-throwers, gas and smoke during the fighting around Fleury in June 1916: 'Inside the shelter was indescribable turmoil, frantic comings and goings, the moans of the wounded, the coughing of the gassed, burning sandbags releasing clouds of acrid fumes that thickened the well-nigh unbreathable atmosphere still further.' The Germans almost effected a breach but were driven off at bayonet point by the men of 22nd Chasseurs and 297th Infantry.

Chapter Five

Sacrifice and Glory

The attack on Fort Souville on 12 July represented the high-water mark of the German advance. On 20 July French forces retook La Poudrière, a position outside the fort, and late July and August saw them regaining ground around Fleury and south of the Ouvrage de Thiaumont. Pétain and Nivelle had worked hard to assemble a strong force from their meagre resources, devoting special attention to the artillery. Both men preferred to use firepower to blast through the enemy defences, rather than infantry to push through them. Nivelle's concept of a 'rolling barrage' was refined, the 75mm guns 'lifting' their fire by 50m every two minutes, while the heavier guns aimed 150m beyond the initial target of the 75s, with lifts of 500m to 1,000m. The infantry would follow as closely as possible behind the barrage, trials suggesting a distance of 50 to 75m. The internal organization of the infantry company was also addressed, adding extra light machine-gunners and bombers, and reducing the number of riflemen.

The man chosen to lead the counter-attack was General Mangin, commander of XI Corps. Characterized as a man who 'breathed energy, daring and a burning hope of promotion', the ex-colonial reminded the writer Henry Bordeaux of 'a wild boar ready to charge'. A brigadier at the start of the war, within a month Mangin had been appointed to command 5th Division; in June 1916 he was promoted again to command XI Corps, and that autumn his units would be at the forefront of efforts to recapture Fort Douaumont.

Using an assault force of just three divisions, supported by 600 guns of all calibres, Mangin was meticulous in his preparations. After an opening bombardment on 17 October, a dummy attack five days later served to locate the enemy batteries, which were then subjected to counter-battery fire before the real offensive got under way the next day. Advancing behind a rolling barrage, lifting 100m every four minutes, the French infantry made gains all along the line. One shell penetrated the roof of Fort Douaumont and exploded in a magazine. Fires broke out and the fort became untenable; the majority of the troops were evacuated, leaving just a handful of pioneers to fight the flames. The following morning, under cover of fog, the assault troops scrambled forward over ground pocked with thousands of craters after the months of shelling. The men of the Régiment Coloniale du Maroc (RICM) and 321st Infantry entered the fort, and by evening the Germans had surrendered. Three desperate counter-attacks were repelled over the next three days, then on 28 October the French turned their bombardment on Fort Vaux and its surrounds. After a five-day battering the Germans withdrew, and the French walked into an empty fort.

Although the French now occupied the key strongholds on the right-bank ridges, it needed a further offensive in December 1916 to evict the Germans from the positions they held in the ground to the north. The terrain was the same shell-cratered chaos faced by the infantry two months earlier, but the Germans had used the intervening period to install extra trenches and deep concrete-lined dug-outs. The French began their bombardment on 11 December and went over the top four days later. Moving forward with élan, the advancing troops took strongpoint after strongpoint, village after village: Vacherauville, Louvemont, Bezonvaux, the Côte du Poivre, Haudromont quarries, Bois des Caurettes – all were recaptured. Over 11,000 Germans were taken prisoner, along with 115 cannon and 170 machine guns.

The offensive marked the last significant action in the Verdun sector until 1917. In August the Germans were finally ejected from their positions on the left bank of the Meuse, although it would take the Franco-American offensive of September 1918 to finally restore the front line of February 1916. But the victory cost France dear. Some 162,440 men were reported killed (61,289) or missing (101,151) at Verdun, almost 10 per cent of the country's total war dead, with another 216,337 wounded. Casualties from the Somme offensive were higher still, more than doubling the number of dead and missing in 1916 to 350,200. Even then, it was by no means the bloodiest year of the First World War – 1914 (454,000) and 1915 (391,000) both exacted a heavier toll – but for the French it is Verdun that symbolizes the conflict. Contemporaries perceived it as a uniquely terrible battle, a view that still holds current today. Nearly three-quarters of the army on the western front served in the sector, and saying 'I was there' united the surviving veterans, turning the battle of Verdun into a shared national experience and the hills above the Meuse into the focus of modern commemoration.

Verdun, 11 June 1916. General Charles Mangin (third from left), commander of XI Corps, and his staff. A former colonial soldier, Mangin soon acquired a reputation as a thruster and was promoted to command XI Corps in June 1916. He attracted much criticism for the losses sustained by his formations, but he remained unyielding: 'You lose a lot of men whatever you do.'

A French command post, La Poudrière, Fort Souville, 25 July 1916. La Poudrière, the powder magazine outside the fort, was retaken by the French on 20 July 1916, the first position to be recaptured from the Germans. The bicycle (left) is intended for use by the runners, who would be lucky indeed if they could ride it across the broken ground.

Fort Saint-Michel, 17 June 1916. Built in 1875, Saint-Michel was another element of the inner defensive ring on the right bank of the Meuse. In February 1916 the fort was virtually unmanned and serving as a headquarters. Here, the Germans are 'about to get what's coming to them' from '*La Ration*', a 105mm gun positioned nearby. In the background are the heights of Froideterre. No two members of the crew are dressed alike: some are wearing regulation horizon blue; others are still in the corduroy uniforms issued in the winter of 1914/15, or in blue canvas barracks dress.

Territorials dig extra trenches around Fort Saint-Michel, 14 October 1916. Sous-lieutenant Albert Texier watched as men from 42nd Infantry dug in near Fort Vaux: 'Sometimes a digger half stands, shocked to the core. He drops his pick and shovel; the ground is full of corpses. "We're digging up flesh, sir!" [he says]. "Take no notice," [comes the reply]. "Just dig!"'

Stretcher bearers attempt to identify a body, Fort Souville, 14 October 1916. 'Helped by the soldiers, the stretcher bearers did their utmost to give a decent burial to those who died at the aid post,' said Quartermaster Sergeant Joseph Méjecaze (14th Infantry). 'But they could only work at night. If the Germans saw earth being turned over, as sometimes happened, they would unleash a violent bombardment that destroyed everything. Men almost always ended up in a mass grave, bodies piled on top of each other. What else could we do? Sometimes the pick got buried in something soft and released a distinctive odour. A body! And the digger had to move aside. How would we identify these human remains later?'

Ouvrage de Thiaumont and its surrounds, 1 July 1916. In this aerial view the ouvrage itself is the irregularity, bottom right. Artilleryman René Vilar watched the German bombardment on 3 August: 'It was one long explosion of shells of all calibres. Between Souville on our left and Thiaumont on our right, tongues of flames and smoke seemed to rise from the ground like a volcano. The earth boiled like water on the hob. During any brief lull, we could see the infantrymen in their shell-holes through our binoculars. My God, what agony! Poor devils!'

Fleury, 2 August 1916. A soldier hurries back to his own lines carrying a German machine gun during the French counter-attack on the village. Some captured weapons were distributed among the divisional machine-gun schools for training purposes so the French could turn enemy guns against their former owners. Machine-gunner Etienne Raynal (81st Infantry) saw 'many wounded men sheltering near the Ouvrage de Thiaumont, thinking they would be safer there, only to be killed by the shells. A shell fell near a wounded man heading in our direction. The explosion flung a part-decomposed body in the air and it came crashing down on top of him. The poor man ran towards us, plastered with human remains. The stench was appalling. There was nothing we could do for him. Find an aid post! we shouted. He came past us screaming and disappeared, probably out of his mind.'

The French attack goes in south of Fleury, 2 August 1916. Machine-gunners move forward, while prisoners scramble back. 'Our prisoner made us understand that he was happy his war was over,' reported Private Suteau (169th Infantry). 'If he'd hesitated so long before surrendering, it was only because the Germans opposite had been told the French kill their prisoners at bayonet point.'

Fleury, 18 August 1916. Men of the Régiment d'Infanterie Coloniale du Maroc (RICM) organize their position in the recaptured village. Romain Darchy (408th Infantry) had watched the village being destroyed: 'The houses collapsed one by one: a wall here, roof timbers there, a thousand tiles shattering, flames licking up the walls, the noise of a thousand things breaking under the avalanche of shells. Now it's just a gigantic chaos of rubble, food, furniture, clothes and books, lost amid the stones. All that remains is a bell tower in danger of collapse and a cemetery with tombs ripped open and crosses smashed.'

Fleury, August 1916. French troops consolidate the former German positions overlooking the village, captured by 342nd Infantry on 23 August 1916. 'There's nothing left of Fleury,' wrote journalist Henry Bordeaux. 'Only a patch paler than the rest flattened against the brown earth like an overripe fruit. Map in hand, a staff officer spouted what seemed like nonsense: "Here's the main street and the church. There's the *mairie*." My eyes sought out the *mairie*, the church and the main street but could find not a trace.'

The remains of the 60cm narrow-gauge military railway between Fleury and the Ouvrage de Thiaumont, 1916. Lines had been installed in France's four eastern fortresses: Verdun, Belfort, Toul and Épinal. The rolling stock was specially developed by Engineer Lieutenant Colonel Prosper Péchot and Engineer Bourdon, from the engine manufacturer Decauville, to handle difficult terrain and reach the hilltop forts. The locos, mainly double Fairlies, employed twin boilers fed from a single central firebox so they could tackle gentle gradients; each could replace up to a hundred horses and pull a payload of 48 tonnes. A civilian line was added to the network in 1914, joining Verdun, Fleury and Vaux to the new Woëvre line from Commercy to Montmédy.

Stretcher bearers collect the wounded, 21 October 1916. The bandsmen in each regiment also doubled up as stretcher bearers. They were supplemented by further 'groups' of sixty bearers, distinguished by their Red Cross armlet, who formed part of each divisional and army corps medical unit.

Clearing casualties from the field, Côte 304. Each divisional stretcher-bearer unit had its own padre, pictured here in dark clothing. 'I scarcely have energy enough to pray,' recalled one Jesuit priest. Although there were no official regimental padres, colonels normally allowed the many priests called into the ranks to minister to their comrades.

Enemy prisoners were also used to carry the wounded to safety. Here a group of Germans wait outside an aid post near Fleury, 18 August 1916. A number have been given French forage caps.

400mm gun, Lemmes, August 1916. Shells from this massive gun – one of just eight manufactured in 1915 – crushed German-held strongpoints, including those at Fort Douaumont and Fort Vaux. On 23 October 1916 six shells penetrated the reinforced concrete of Fort Douaumont: one exploded in a magazine, rendering the position untenable and forcing the Germans to evacuate most of the troops sheltering there. The RICM attacked and took the fort the following day.

Fort Douaumont, 25 October 1916. Having recaptured the ruined fort, these men of the RICM are sheltering close to the western Bourges casemate, the perimeter wall behind them. First into the fort were a mixture of colonials from 8th Battalion RICM and their supporting engineers, 19/2 Field Company. According to Engineer Sergeant Fernand Ducom, the Germans surrendered to 'a crafty little fixer from the Paris *banlieu*', one Artificer Sergeant Dumont, who managed to 'con the four officers and twenty-four men, all pioneers, the whole garrison at the time of the attack'.

The wreck of a French aircraft near Fort Douaumont, 25 October 1916. The plane flew too low in the mist while on a contact patrol in support of the attacking infantry. During 1916 the aviation service lost 759 men killed or missing on the Western Front, 16 per cent of its total losses during the conflict. But just four in every ten were killed in action; the rest met their deaths in accidents at the front or in training.

Fort Douaumont, 25 October 1916. Laden with water and ammunition, a carrying party from a colonial regiment tramps uphill to the fort.

The victorious troops of the RICM await their pick-up on 30 October 1916. The chance for a well-merited rest came not a moment too soon for Timothée Méléra: 'Woke up curled in a ball, stiff as a stump. My head was heavy as lead. A kind of stupefied calm has descended. Covered in mud from head to toe.... It's thirty-six hours since the attack and my memories are already a blur. All that's left is a sort of numb horror.'

Fort Douaumont, 26 December 1916. An aid post within the recaptured fort, well stocked with bandages and bottles of medicine (left). The duty orderly smokes a cigarette, while behind him the doctor treats a wound. In line with pre-war theory, French army doctors were expecting to deal primarily with bullet wounds, but in practice the majority of injuries were inflicted by shells to the upper torso and head.

Fort Douaumont, 27 December 1916. Troops shelter in one of the galleries. Engineer Sergeant Ducom had received orders in October to put the recaptured fort in a state of defence: 'Simple sergeant that I am, this cost me a violent altercation with a major from 102nd Infantry. They had arrived to relieve 1st Battalion RICM and persisted in blocking the corridors rather than occupy their designated positions in front of the fort. My forceful manner eventually persuaded him to leave.'

Fort Belleville, 27 October 1916. A welcome drink for this Chauchat light machine-gun team, recently out of the front line. Mud – *glaise* – afflicted the combatants even in the height of summer. 'I came down from the front line this morning,' Captain Georges Gallois (221st Infantry) wrote to his parents. 'I was just one big clod of mud. I had to grab a knife and scrape my clothes before I could drag myself further, the skirts of my greatcoat were plastered to my legs with mud. I was thirsty rather than hungry … [and] dropping from fatigue.'

Ouvrage Adalbert, 24 December 1916. Stretcher bearers prepare to evacuate a badly wounded casualty, several wearing sheepskins to help ward off the cold. The Ouvrage Adalbert was officially TD2, one of the chain of small redoubts lying between the Ouvrage de Thiaumont and Fort Douaumont. The Germans captured TD2 on 21 June 1916 and established a position there. It was heavily bombarded by the French and subsequently recaptured on 24 October 1916.

Ouvrage Adalbert, December 1916. Stretches of track from the 60cm narrow-gauge railway serving the forts were also used to move casualties. Here, two more German prisoners have been pressed into service as orderlies.

The railway was also employed to bring up supplies and ammunition. Here, corrugated iron and sandbags are being used to consolidate the newly recaptured ground.

Near the Ouvrage Adalbert, 25 October 1916. Digging a communications trench to connect Batterie F with the newly recaptured Fort Douaumont.

13th Brigade HQ, redoubt MF4, east of the Ouvrage de Froideterre, 21 October 1916. General Léon Farret, commander of 13th Brigade, offers a light to one of his men. After a month out of the lines, the brigade was just beginning its second tour of duty in the sector, where it would remain until 14 December 1916. Farret – 'small, stout, pince-nez, an ex-colonial', according to his former lieutenant, Charles Delvert – had led 101st Infantry at the battle of Ethe in August 1914. He took command of 13th Brigade the following month and stayed with it until the infantry reorganization of 1917.

Improving the defences around trench redoubt MF3, south of the Ouvrage de Froideterre, November 1916. Although numbered in sequence with the two pre-war *abris* constructed between Fort Saint-Michel and Froideterre, MF3 was built during the battle.

Belleville. A ruined house conceals a camouflaged naval 164mm gun. Two of these 164s, part of 1st Mobile Battery under Lieutenant de Vaisseau Lecour Grandmaison, arrived in November 1916 to supplement the 140mm naval guns already serving at Verdun. The second 164mm gun was located at the Ferme du Cabaret, east of the city. Although serving on land, the gun crew still wear the wide-collared naval jumper, but they have swapped their *bachi* caps for steel helmets.

A battery of 120mm guns is well concealed in dug-outs covered by groundsheets in the Bois des Trois Cornes. The 'wood' lay just behind the front line, between the Ouvrage de Froideterre and the Ouvrage de Thiaumont, but remained in French hands throughout the fighting. Even with air superiority, guns were always vulnerable to spotter planes, hence the need for camouflage.

Near the Abri des Quatre Cheminées, 25 October 1916. A 65mm mountain gun fires on Fort Vaux. Originally introduced in 1906, the gun could be broken down into three parts for transport by mule. It was an accurate weapon, capable of firing up to fifteen rounds a minute, with a range of 5,500m.

Fort Vaux. An aerial view of the recaptured fort. On the night of 3 November 1916, Lieutenant Diot and a mixed party from 118th Infantry and 13/63 Field Company made their careful way into the fort, expecting an ambush or trap. Once inside, 'an unbearable stench caught them by the throat: a mixture of smoke, gas and decay. A grim sight confronted them: rubbish still burning, fragments of grenades, used cartridge cases, nameless debris, the detritus of war. Two or three bodies lay in a corridor, bathed in a flickering light by the dying embers of a brazier.'

Fort Vaux, 22 November 1916. A group of Engineers squeeze into some cramped accommodation within the recaptured fort. Journalist Henry Bordeaux and his companions had visited a couple of weeks earlier: 'Down one flight of steps, up another, and we were inside. The corridors have been partly cleared but are still cluttered with German metal-sprung bunk beds … All the flanking casemates have been destroyed, except that in the south-west corner, which can easily be repaired. One of the galleries has been blown up … But it was reassuring to see inside the fort. The barracks are already clean and organized and the passages have been tidied up.'

Fort Vaux, 22 November. A Saint-Etienne machine gun has been installed in one of the flanking Bourges casemates of the recaptured fort. The fort had been so badly damaged by the constant shelling that its 75mm gun turret proved impossible to repair. The turret was removed in 1917 and replaced with an armoured machine-gun nest. The remaining 75s, located in the Bourges casemates, had been removed by the Germans, leaving the fort with two pom-poms and twenty-two machine guns, heavy and light.

Runners arrive at Fort Vaux, 22 November. With telephone lines vulnerable to shelling, and visual signalling to smoke and dust, runners remained the most reliable form of battlefield communication. They often travelled in pairs in case one was killed or wounded. 'I enjoyed my job as a runner,' said Louis Foucault (120th Chasseurs). 'The confidence placed in us and our pleasure in overcoming the dangers we faced were ample reward for my efforts.'

Canal de l'Est, 12 July 1916. Men watch from barges as German prisoners are moved to the rear under cavalry escort. 'German prisoners marched by,' remembered Doctor Léon Baros (217th Infantry). 'We bandaged their wounds as they passed. They were hungry and thirsty, faces drawn, uniforms muddy and tattered. They begged us for something to eat and drink. And our soldiers, who had just suffered so much at their hands, set aside all animosity and in a great wave of generosity gave them bread, chocolate and water. The men we bandaged wept and offered us everything they had: penknives, cigars [and] matchboxes.'

Captured ground on Côte 378, south-east of Louvemont, December 1916. Côte 378 and the neighbouring Côte 342 fell easily on 15 December 1916 to the troops of 38th Division (8th Tirailleurs, 4th Zouaves, 4th Mixed Zouaves and Tirailleurs, and RICM). The men pressed on to take Louvemont, advancing again the following day before the attack petered out: '[That's when] our ordeal really began,' recalled Bastien Feice (4th Zouaves). 'The snow that had been falling non-stop for two days gave way to the most intense cold. The temperature fell to −20°. By dawn, those spared by shot and shell were no longer men, but frozen, muddy, almost lifeless forms. Nearly everyone was suffering from frostbite: some in the feet, some in the hands, many with both legs frozen. I suffered first-degree frostbite in both feet. It took me almost four hours to cover the 1,500 metres separating me from the aid post.'

Sunken barges in the Canal de l'Est formed a convenient bridge for troops to advance and retake the village of Vacherauville at bayonet point on 15 December 1916. While still afloat, the barges had served as billets. 'There was nothing pleasant about life on these barges,' claimed Maurice Sambon, a machine-gunner in 105th Infantry. 'In mid-August we were living in the depths of the hold, penned in like animals, along with the lice and fleas infesting the planks. The heat was unbearable. To cap it all, the 105s kept landing in the Meuse beside us. We expected to be waking up at any minute on the river bed.'

Major Thinus and the officers of 3rd Battalion, 112th Infantry (126th Division). They include Captain Maigrot and Captain Onofri, the two company commanders who retook Vacherauville, capturing 300 prisoners. Eight Frenchmen were killed and forty-five wounded. The regiment held the village for eight days before being relieved.

Second Army HQ, Souilly, 9 November 1916. The battle of Verdun quickly acquired an epic quality that attracted many foreign visitors. In a medals ceremony in front of Second Army HQ at the *mairie* in Souilly, a French soldier is congratulated by HRH Prince Arthur of Connaught. A number of men appear to have received the Military Medal, while the staff officer on the right sports the Military Cross. General Nivelle stands on the right, facing the camera. Note also the Wallace fountain far right.

Second Army HQ, Souilly, September 1916. Another famous visitor was the British minister of war, David Lloyd George (centre, donning his overcoat). Lloyd George had arrived to present the city with the Military Cross and gave a speech at a dinner in the citadel: 'The memory of the victorious resistance of Verdun will be immortal, because Verdun saved, not only France, but the whole of our great cause which is common to ourselves and humanity. I bring to you a tribute of the admiration of my country, of the great Empire which I represent here. They bow with me before your sacrifice and before your glory. Once again, for the defence of the great causes with which its very future is bound up, mankind turns to France.' Also present was writer Henry Bordeaux, then attached to the staff. Even the English speakers found it hard to follow Lloyd George's Welsh accent, he reported, '[but] we had no need to understand his words to know that his theme was sacrifice and glory.'